# Pauline's Book for Girls

# Pauline's Book for Girls

STEVE COOGAN AND HENRY NORMAL

Hodder & Stoughton

First published in Great Britain in 1996 by Hodder and Stoughton
A division of Hodder Headline PLC

10  9  8  7  6  5  4  3  2  1

British Library Cataloguing in Publication Data
A CIP catalogue record for this title is available from the British Library

ISBN   0 340 68066 0

**Design and artwork** by THE BRIDGEWATER BOOK COMPANY
**Designers:** Peter Bridgewater and John Christopher
**Illustration:** Paul Allen, Paul Collicut, Ivan Hissey, Kurt Hoyte,
Mainline Design, Fred Pipes, and Curtis Tappenden
**Steve Coogan's wardrobe by** Marcia Stanton
**Steve Coogan's make-up and styling by** Lisa Cavalli-Green

GRATEFUL ACKNOWLEDGMENTS TO:
Geoff Posner, Dave Tyler, John Thompson, Patrick Marber, Sandra Gough, Sally Rogers,
Lisa Cavalli-Green, Marcia Stanton, John Wood, Jan Murphy, Angela Pell, John Hannah

Printed and bound in Great Britain by
Butler & Tanner Ltd, Frome and London

Hodder and Stoughton
A division of Hodder Headline PLC
338 Euston Road
London NW1 3BH

# Dedicated To
## Barbra Streisand

*an inspiration to*
*big-boned women everywhere*

# Contents

Steve Coogan & Henry Normal

pauline's
CD for Girls

HODDER HEADLINE AUDIOBOOKS

sex problems solved!

pauline's 101 celebrity exploits

One CD • Playing time approx 1 hour

**12** Monday — Found a dead rabbit by the roadside. All its gibblets were hanging out. I got home & after Animal Magic I cried. Paul said I should have broke its neck - to make sure it were dead. Apparently that's what they do in the army. Anyway he said they were a pest. Bob was nice to me, he said there was no chance of them becoming extinct as they breed like rabbits. Then he suggested I should have brought it home & cooked it in a pie. He says they're a delicacy in France.

I ♡ DARREN

DARREN IS A TWAT!!

**13** Tuesday — Paul said Emperor Hirohito used to eat them live for breakfast. I think he's probably making it up.

> Today Louise Cooper said that she thought I was doing myself no favours by cheeking the teachers & that the rest of the class was being held back.
> I had to smack her!

**14** Wednesday — We had double history today with Miss Boarshaw. She's got a moustache & smells like burnt sprouts. She never does anything with her hair.
Julie reckons she's a lesbian!!
We're doing Weimar Germany at the moment. They had wheelbarrows full of money & people would steal the wheelbarrows & leave

Miss Boarshaw

**15** Thursday — the money. Imagine that! A packet of fags would cost about £5,000! I'd hate to have lived then, having to talk German all the time & with my Saturday job I couldn't afford to buy anything. Miss Boarshaw offered me a lift home in her car.
NO WAY! I know what she's after...

Louise Cooper came up & said she was
sorry today. I showed her how to cover up her
black eye with some of my foundation & powder.
She's offered to do my homework next week.

Julie says Miss Boarshaw has lesbian orgies ALL the
time at her house. Theresa McBreen says miss
Boarshaw has them every Wednesday & that she'd
seen LOADS of women with short hair going round
there and not leaving till after midnight.

Paul said it was all vicious rumours & you shouldn't
make allegations unless somebody has seen it for
themselves. He then immediately volunteered to
"see it for himself" — He said it was the only
honourable thing to do.

Got at games & went down the Arndale Centre—
We had a right laugh.

Paul kept going on & on about the unspeakable
sex orgy he'd seen through Miss Boarshaw's living-room
window. Paul says she was like an animal. He said
they seemed to be possessed by the Devil. They
danced around NAKED before performing what he
described as a "lesbian voodoo sex ritual".

 I bumped into Fat Bob on the way home.
His account was very different. He said " 8 women
arrived & sat in a circle on chairs & chatted for
about 3 hours." He said, "at one point miss
Boarshaw went out of the room & returned 5 minutes
later with a tray of biscuits at which point Paul
just got up & went home.

**19** Monday  Just come back from seeing Duran Duran in concert. Simon Le Bon is __fantastic__. I love the way he pushes the sleeves up on his jacket & struts his stuff. He wears a bandana & white towelling socks, probably because he sweats so much on stage. He took off his T shirt & flung it into the crowd. I had to smack about 3 girls to get hold of it. In the end I just got a sleeve. It's got some blood on it, but I don't think it's his.

**20** Tuesday  Theresa McBreen likes Roger Taylor, the drummer. She can have him! He's alright, but all he does is sit there drumming. The best one is John Taylor, the bass-player. You can tell he's dead sensitive & shy— he just sways from side to side & occasionally just looks up all sheepish. At one point he looked up and gave a cheeky smile & I swear to God he was

**21** Wednesday  looking at me. I think he must be telepathic because it was exactly at the moment I was imagining showing my tits to him. I sometimes dream about him, I wonder if he dreams about me.

On the way home stopped off at the chippy. I was "hungry like the wolf!"

**22** Thursday  Julie says she fancies our Paul. When he was out I took her in his bedroom and showed her his underpants drawer. There were none in there.— She said "Where are they?" I said "He's only got one pair— and he's wearing them".

Dad might have to have his lung removed.
He's cursing & can't believe his bad luck. He's
just bought 200 duty free Rothman's but Paul put
them out of his reach. Paul said he refused to stand
by & watch his father kill himself, then offered to take
the whole lot off his hands for 2 quid.

Julie's <u>still</u> fancying our Paul! She says she
used to fancy Patrick MacDonald but she saw Paul
batter him & now she's got a thing for Paul.
He's enjoying himself at the moment. He's cock of the
estate, but only until next week when my knight
in shining armour, Barry Parry, comes out of Risley
Remand

P.C.
&
B.P.

Life is <u>so</u> depressing. It rained <u>all</u> day.
I saw on the news some old woman in London
got beaten up for 60p. If I were going to beat
someone up I'd want a lot more than that
for my troubles.

We got a new geography teacher today, Mr. Tierney, he
is <u>gorgeous</u>. He's got hair like David Essex. He wears
a leather jacket and likes Genesis. I put some make up
on in the bogs at dinner time. We had him for last
lesson so I asked if I could talk to him after class.
I walked right up to him, threw my arms round
him & burst into tears. I said I didn't understand
about sedimentary deposits. Nothing happened —
but he was sweating — I
could smell it.

MR TIERNEY
&
LOVES
PAULINE

Saw Mr. Tierney again today, he
won't look me in the eye.
Dirty bastard — I know what he's after . . .
He'll get it and all.

# I slept with my lover's dad and his grandad – now all three are dead

## ...and I am deaf in one ear.

## Pauline's true story

I met Carl when he was working as a pizza delivery boy. One day he came round with a meat feast. He seemed shy and vulnerable. As the weeks progressed I found myself going through the entire menu of speciality pizzas. Then one day he came round with a Mexican hot which he gave to me free as it was a cancelled order. I was ravenous. Afterwards he offered himself for dessert. He parked his scooter and came inside. After that, it was deep pan every night.

It was like a fairytale romance. We went to the pictures, tenpin bowling and the swimming baths, and with his contacts, food was never a problem. Somehow I knew it was too good to be true, it couldn't last forever.

One day during the long hot summer, I called in at Pablo's Pizzas. A stranger answered the door. He was tall and Mediterranean looking, and when our eyes met the atmosphere was electric – you could cut it with a knife. 'Aye,' he said, as he stretched out his firm, masculine hand, 'I'm Pablo'. He showed me round the kitchen with an air of confidence. He knew where everything went. I was spellbound as he masterfully grated mozzarella onto a cheese supreme. He let me toss his doughballs.

That afternoon we made love everywhere – on the chopping table, up against the ovens, in his van. Later on, as we hosed each other down, I said, 'You're like a much more mature version of Carl.' He mumbled something about, 'It runs in the family.' 'What do you mean?' I said. 'Didn't you know?' he replied, 'CARL IS MY SON.' I was gobsmacked.

Later that evening I met Carl at Froggies Fun Pub. He wanted to go and see *Passenger 57* starring Wesley Snipes, whereas I wanted to see *Three Men and a Little Lady* again. It turned into a blazing row. Eventually we decided to go back to my place, but as we kissed and made up he ran his fingers through my hair and found a piece of uncooked ground beef. 'What's this?' he said. 'I don't know, it must be from the pizza we had earlier,' I spluttered. 'But that was a Hawaiian,' he replied, 'they only come with ham, pineapple and mushrooms. And besides, this ground beef is uncooked. The only place you can find this is in the kitchen of my father's pizza parlour.' A tear trickled down his face as he looked into my soul. He knew the truth. I could not lie. 'I'm so sorry,' I replied. 'I couldn't stop myself.' He went very quiet. He seemed to be in a trance as he turned and walked from the pub like a man possessed. It was about midnight when I heard a knock on the door. That knock still echoes in me like a bell. It was the police. Apparently Carl had beaten his father to death with a pastry mallet and then taken his own life by driving his scooter into the path of an Intercity 125 near Stockport Viaduct. After the impact the only thing that could be identified was his crash-helmet which bore the logo "Pablo and Son". His head was still inside the helmet. Clenched between his teeth was a note which read, 'I'm so sorry, I couldn't help myself.' The policeman said his remains looked like uncooked ground beef. It chilled me to the bone.

At the family funeral, the church was packed with suppliers and customers. Pablo's father had flown all the way from Palermo in Sicily. He was 85, tanned, with silver hair like a punch-drunk Blake Carrington. We both needed a shoulder to cry on and inevitably that evening we ended up in bed together. At three o'clock in the morning the grief was too much for him and he had a heart attack. Many believe I came out of the whole tragedy unscathed. No one will ever know the emotional and mental scars I carry, not to mention being partially deaf due to an ear infection I caught due to the stress of the whole palaver. I know one thing, I will never again order pizza, but if I do, it will be a vegi-max, a seafood or a calypso, as none of these have ground beef.

**that afternoon we made love ever**

12

ere...

**14**

# BE AS FIT AS A BUTCHER'S DOG
# SEXERCISE

THE SEXERCISE PROGRAMME is to be undertaken entirely at your own risk. Pauline accepts no responsibility for physical or sociological injuries howsoever incurred.

# WORKOUT ROUTINE

### CHICKEN WINGS

Sit on top. Elbows up, deep breath,
do bust exercises.

### REVERSE BARROW BOY

Get into reverse wheelbarrow
position, arms straight. Do sit ups.

### BIG BIRD

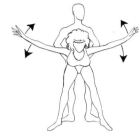

Stand in front, legs apart. Bend
forward, flap arms rhythmically.

### THE BIKE

Lay down flat on back, arms out-
stretched, bicycling legs.

### HEADMASTER

Keeping legs straight, bend from
the waist and touch toes.

### TEASEMAID

With legs together, and arms
supported, dip and push.

### BOAT RACE

Kneel with legs apart and
row in and out.

### STARFISH

Place feet wide apart, raise arms
and imitate starfish.

### CRAB CATCHER

Squat with legs apart and arms
wide and push down.

### BARROW BOY

Get into standard wheelbarrow
position and do press ups.

### NODDING DOG

Kneel on fours and nod head
up and down.

### BOA CONSTRICTOR

Sit with one leg bent and one leg
extended and twist from the waist.

GIRLS' TALK
# 0001 BOYFRIENDS
JONATHAN ROSS IS DEAD **SOPHISTICATED**.

# 101 CELEBRITY SEXPLOITS

THIS LIST IS BY NO MEANS EXHAUSTIVE. THOSE OMITTED SHOULD NOT TAKE OFFENCE.

| NAME | LOCATION | COMMENTS | SYMBOL |
|---|---|---|---|
| KEN RUSSELL | FARM | *A sick man.* | ❣❣❣❣ |
| JONATHAN ROSS | CECIL GEES | *He said he was just trying it on. A snug fit it was.* | ✿ ○ |
| RICHARD WHITELY | TRAVEL LODGE | *He said, 'I'll have two from the top and one from the bottom'.* | ↑↓ |
| JOHN McVICAR | SOHO | *Not as hard as he looks.* | ✿ |
| STEVE COOGAN | JUMBO JET | *Sensitive, passionate, imaginative, perfect.* | ○○○ |
| ROBERT ROBERTSON | THE GARRICK CLUB | *I called his bluff.* | ○ |
| DAVID DIMBLEBY | BBC CANTEEN | *The embodiment of professional broadcasting. A tit man.* | ✿ |
| JONATHAN DIMBLEBY | BBC CANTEEN | *Like two peas in a pod and his brother was no different.* | ✿ |
| RICHARD MADELEY | HOLIDAY INN, COPTHORNE B'HAM | *Smooth as an eel. Big feet.* | ✿ |
| SEAN BEAN | HIS FLAT | *Wore Sheffield Wednesday kit but still managed to score.* | ✿ |
| DAVID MELLOR | THE THISTLE, BRIGHTON | *Lost his deposit.* | ❣ |
| RORY BREMNER | EDINBURGH FESTIVAL | *Kept doing impressions of Frank Bruno, but made love like Frank Spencer. 'Oooh Betty I've come'.* | ✿ |
| BARRY NORMAN | BBC CANTEEN | *He just wanted to watch.* | ❣ |
| PAULA YATES | TOILETS AT BHS | *This proves the myth, you can't teach an old dog new tricks.* | ○❣❣ |
| MICHAEL WINNER | KITCHEN AT THE CAPPRICE | *Loser* | ↑ |
| TERRY CHRISTIAN | ARNDALE CENTRE | *Virgin* | ✿ |
| CHRIS EVANS | GROUCHO CLUB | *Evans above…and below.* | ✿ |
| CHARLIE DRAKE | DAVENPORT THEATRE, STOCKPORT | *Knocked me out. Then he had sex with me.* | ❣ |
| JIM DAVIDSON | HMS BELFAST | *Brewers droop. A disaster.* | ↓ |
| THE KRANKIES | BUTLINS, SKEGNESS | *Rubber bedsheets. Very weird.* | ❣❣❣❣ |
| PAUL DANIELS | THE LONDON SAVOY | *I like it…not a lot…but I liked it.* | ↑ |
| BILLY BRAGG | TENT AT GLASTONBURY | *Kept saying, 'You love it, you slag'.* | ○ |
| MICK HUCKNALL | GMEX | *Simply dead.* | ✿ |
| CHRIS DE BURGH | TOILET, HEATHROW DEPARTURES | *I made him sing, unfortunately.* | ↑ |
| IAN McSHANE | NORFOLK BROADS | *Enjoyed sitting on his barge.* | ✿❣ |
| OLIVER TOBIAS | CARAVANETTE, DORSET | *Tried to sell me pegs.* | ↑↓ |
| MR MOTIVATOR | KINTBURY HEALTH-HYDROME | *Like a traction engine in lycra.* | ○ |
| GARY LINEKER | METROPOLE B'HAM NEC | *Dirty bastard.* | ❣❣❣○○ |
| PAUL GASCOIGNE | FIVE BELLIES' HOUSE | *I made him cry.* | ✿ |
| RYAN GIGGS | LAGITANNE | *The boy done good.* | ✿ |
| PETER STRINGFELLOW | STRINGFELLOWS | *Who'd have thought it, 55 this year, 56 if you include me.* | ✿ |
| IAN BOTHAM | COTTAGE IN YEOVIL | *Howzat!* | ❣ |
| MICHAEL FISH | BBC CANTEEN | *Fillet o'fish with a tartar sauce. Hmmmm.* | ○ ❣❣ |

❣ **KINKY**   ✿ **FULL SHAG**   ↑ **TOPS**   ↑↓ **TOPS AND DOWNSTAIRS**   ○ **ORGASM**

| NAME | LOCATION | COMMENTS | SYMBOL |
|------|----------|----------|--------|
| PRINCE NASEEM | STRETCH LIMO, BRADFORD | *Won on points.* | ✪ ○ |
| JOE BUGNER | BACK OF THE BLUE MARLIN FISH RESTAURANT | *Stopped due to cut above his left eye.* | ↑↓ |
| WILL CARLING | SWALLOW HOTEL, BRISTOL | *Nice tackle.* | ✪ |
| THE MARQUIS OF BLANDFORD | PARTY AT BARRY GIBB'S HOUSE | *The Marquis de Sade* | ↑ |
| STEVE DAVIS | PARTY AT BARRY GIBB'S HOUSE | *Up against the cushion.* | ✪ |
| STEPHEN HENDRY | HIS MUM'S HOUSE | *What a palava.* | ↑ |
| JOHN McCRIRICK | STABLES, CHEPSTOW | *Almost put off by the smell.* | ✪ |
| KILROY SILK | THE ADONIS SOLARIUM, COVENTRY | *Turned over half way through to get an even tan.* | ✪ |
| EAMONN HOLMES | PARTY AT BARRY GIBB'S HOUSE | *Bit chubby.* | ↑↓ |
| NOEL GALLAGHER | OASIS TOUR BUS | *Wonderpants* | ○ |
| LIAM GALLAGHER | OASIS TOUR BUS | *He was mad for it.* | ○ |
| DAMON FROM BLUR | REGENTS PARK ZOO | *He was like an animal, like a ferret up a gutter.* | ✪ |
| NICK BERRY | WINNEBAGO, YORKSHIRE DALES | *Watersports* | ❣❣ |
| STAN BOARDMAN | EMBASSY CLUB, MANCHESTER | *Never put his pint down.* | ✪ |
| JOHN LESLIE | BBC CANTEEN | *Like a blind cobbler's thumb.* | ❣ |
| WOLF | BACK OF HIS RANGE ROVER | *Pretended to be a wolf, very embarrassing.* | ↑↓ |
| MIKE READ DJ | PARTY AT BARRY GIBB'S HOUSE | *Said he loved me!* | ↑ |
| MIKE REID (EASTENDERS) | PARTY AT BARRY GIBB'S HOUSE | *Tried to hold his stomach in, but I gave up.* | ↑↓ |
| SHANE RICHIE | LONDON TO MANCHESTER INTERCITY (FIRST CLASS) | *He got off at Stoke.* | ✪✪✪ |
| ANDREW NEIL | TRAMPS NIGHTCLUB | *Kept saying he was on the telly during sex.* | ✪ |
| MARTIN AMIS | PARTY AT BARRY GIBB'S HOUSE | *Said I was more tangible than posh birds.* | ❣ |
| SALMAN RUSHDIE | PARTY AT BARRY GIBB'S HOUSE | *Said his name was Barry. Very quick.* | ✪ |
| GARY RHODES | BLACK CAB | *He liked them sunny side up.* | ↑ |
| DR HILARY JONES | BBC CANTEEN/MY FLAT/SCRATCHWOOD SERVICES | *Said I had to be taken three times a week.* | ✪✪✪ |
| NIGEL KENNEDY | ROYAL FESTIVAL HALL | *Could only get his hair to stand up.* | ↑ |
| MICHAEL HUTCHENCE | PHONEBOX | *Said we had to be discreet.* | ✪ |
| GARY KEMP | WINE BAR, IPSWICH | *Unkempt* | ✪ |
| ALVIN STARDUST | WIGAN | *Oooh ooh my cooka choo. Disappointing.* | ✪ |
| DAVID ESSEX | JACUZZI AT LONDON HILTON | *Kept calling me Paulette.* | ↑↓ |
| PAUL NICHOLAS | DOMINION THEATRE | *I was glued to my seat.* | ❣ |
| IMRAN KHAN | PARTY AT BARRY GIBB'S | *Imran Khan't.* | ↑ |
| PETER GABRIEL | CHIPPING NORTON RECORDING STUDIOS | *Nice bloke, took me for a pub lunch.* | ✪ |
| ROBERT PALMER | HIS SWISS CHALET | *Short and grumpy, and so was he.* | ✪ |
| CRAIG McLACHLAN | DOMINION THEATRE | *Complete waste of my time and his.* | ↑ |

**❣ KINKY    ✪ FULL SHAG    ↑ TOPS    ↑↓ TOPS AND DOWNSTAIRS    ○ ORGASM**

| NAME | LOCATION | COMMENTS | SYMBOL |
|---|---|---|---|
| DUDLEY MOORE | AT BARRY GIBB'S PARTY | *Raised a smile but that's about all.* | ↑ |
| KEN LIVINGSTONE | AT BARRY GIBB'S PARTY | *Now I know why they call him Red Ken.* | ♥ |
| MARK THATCHER | CAN'T REMEMBER | *I think he wore a cravat.* | ✿ |
| BRIAN MAY | ROGER DALTREY'S FISH FARM | *Lovely hair.* | ✿✿ |
| ROGER DALTREY | HIS FISH FARM | *He said it was 'this big'.* | ↑↓ |
| GORDON BROWN | BRIGHTON CONFERENCE | *A big softy, a bit too much of a softy.* | ↑ |
| JOHN REDWOOD | B AND B, SWANSEA | *Had a leather tawse in an antique velvet case!* | ♥ |
| SEBASTIAN COE | SOUTHPORT SAND DUNES | *Had to wait until he'd plucked his nasal hairs.* | ✿ |
| TONY HATCH | ON A LILO IN CORFU | *He said it was all or nothing. He was half right.* | ↑ |
| LENNY KRAVITZ | HIS AUNTIE'S BUNGALOW | *Flapped his leather coat about like a bat.* | ♥ |
| EARTH, WIND AND FIRE (THE DRUMMER) | COLUMBIA HOTEL, BAYSWATER | *Cream of the crop.* | OOO |
| DAMIEN HIRST | DEWHURSTS | *Innovative* | ♥♥♥ |
| MICHAEL ASPEL | WARDROBE DEPT., LWT | *This is your shag.* | ✿ |
| ROBERT POWELL | THE NEW FOREST | *In a rush to get his hire car back.* | ✿ |
| BOB HOLNESS | HIGHGATE CEMETRY | *A real gentleman, but needs to cut his nails.* | ♥ |
| CLIVE JAMES | IN HIS JAG | *Wanted to marry me.* | ✿ |
| KEITH FLOYD | ROYAL TV SOCIETY AWARDS | *Took his trousers off, then fell asleep.* | ↑ |
| JEREMY CLARKSON | MILLBROOK TEST TRACK | *Pulled off in a lay by.* | ↑↓ |
| FRANK BOUGH | TERRACED HOUSE, ISLINGTON | *A real professional.* | O |
| DICKIE DAVIES | MY BEDROOM | *I showed him a world of sport.* | ✿ |
| GARY NUMAN | BARTON AERODROME | *Still wearing tucker boots.* | ✿ |
| STUART HALL | BBC CANTEEN (MANCHESTER) | *That laugh.* | ↑↓ |
| DESMOND MORRIS | IKEA, WARRINGTON | *Like a bloody animal.* | ✿ |
| LENNIE BENNETT | ROLLS ROYCE | *Hair like a Brillo Pad. Scoured my legs.* | ✿ |
| THE PROCLAIMERS | WOOLWICH FERRY CAR DECK | *I couldn't see where one started and the other one finished.* | O |
| DAVID BAILEY | CHEDDAR GORGE | *He said he'd ring me.* | ✿ |
| MICHAEL DOUGLAS | FIRST CLASS TRANSFER LOUNGE, HEATHROW | *One good Yank.* | ♥ |
| ROBBIE FROM TAKE THAT | TOILETS, BROWN'S NIGHTCLUB | *Take that and that and that.* | OOO |
| KRISS AKABUSI | BACK OF PAUL DANIELS' ROLLS ROYCE | *He wasn't the only one laughing.* | ↑ |
| EDDIE LARGE | WATER RATS CLUB DINNER | *A breach of the Trade Descriptions Act.* | ↑↓ |
| BARRY SHEENE | T.T. ISLE OF MAN | *Fell off a couple of times.* | ✿ |
| JEREMY PAXMAN | BBC DRESSING ROOM | *Probed me extensively.* | OO |
| FRANK SKINNER/DAVID BADDIEL | THEIR PLACE | *Filthy bastards.* | OOO |

**♥ KINKY   ✿ FULL SHAG   ↑ TOPS   ↑↓ TOPS AND DOWNSTAIRS   O ORGASM**

STALLION SHEART

PAULETTE VACHE

# CHAPTER ONE

## In which our heroine meets her match

Her name was Polly Lamb, she was blonde, petite, a size eight. But with a proud bosom that seemed to defy gravity, where weary travellers would oft rest their weary heads. She was the inn-keeper's daughter, in the Travellers Lodge, up near Hatfield. One day a tall, dark stranger alighted from a black stallion in the courtyard. He seemed to dance across the cobbles. It was a delicious dance, a daring dance, a dirty dance. Polly took his coat, noticing it was made of cashmere and from Next For Men. His name was written on the label - Lord Patrick of Swayze.

Their eyes met and without further ado she took him to her bedchamber, reached inside his roughshod breaches and there discovered his stallion-like manhood. Within forty minutes and five he had shot his load thrice-fold. At last, thought Polly, I have met a man who is dead sophisticated. I shall endeavour to get to know him methinks.

# GIRLS' TALK

I'VE BEEN ALL OVER THE WORLD, ME. **I LOVE CULTURE.** I'VE BEEN TO LANZAROTE, BENIDORM, IBIZA, MAJORCA.

NICARAGUA - THAT WERE CRAP - FULL OF STUDENTS PICKING COFFEE BEANS.

**F 6**
SIMPLY THE BEST
*Tina Turner*

**G 7**
BEN
*Michael Jackson*

**H 8**
TOTAL ECLIPSE OF THE HEART
*Bonnie Tyler*

**J 9**
WHEN A MAN LOVES A WOMAN
*Michael Bolton*

**K 10**
I WILL ALWAYS LOVE YOU
*Whitney Houston*

F    G    H    J    K
6    7    8    9    10

# PAULINE'S *Wedding*

## PAINTING BY NUMBERS

### COLOUR KEY

1. FLESH
2. CERISE (LIPSTICK PINK)
3. WHITE
4. CARNATION PINK
5. MAUVE
6. PALE GREEN
7. RED
8. DARK CERISE
9. DARK MAUVE
10. BLONDE
11. DARK BROWN
12. GREY
13. GOLDEN BROWN
14. FAWN
15. REDHEAD RED
16. BROWN

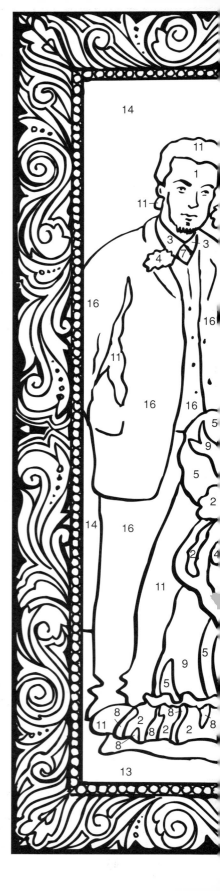

29

POOR OLD UNCLE PAUL

A BOOK FOR PETULA

PAULINE CALF

Paul gets out of bed.
He is very sad. He can't find
his fags.

'Where are my fags?' says
Uncle Paul. 'I'm dying for a
bleedin' fag.'

'I know where they are',
says Paul. 'They're under
the cushion.'

But under the cushion there
was just a piece of toast.

'I know where they are', says
Grandma. 'They're on top of
the telly.'

But on top of the telly there
was just a video.

'I know where they are', says Fat Bob. 'They're in your jacket pocket.'

But in Paul's jacket pocket there was just a chip fork.

'I know where they are',
says Mummy. 'They're
next to the 'phone, you
dopey git.'

But next to the 'phone was
just a pile of empty cans.

'I know where they are', says lovely little Petula. 'Don't you remember? You smoked them all last night when you were on the 'phone to Julie, crying.'

Shut it, you cheeky little cow' says Uncle Paul. Suddenly he gives a big smile and says, 'It doesn't matter, I can make a fag from all these dimps.' Then Uncle Paul goes back to bed.

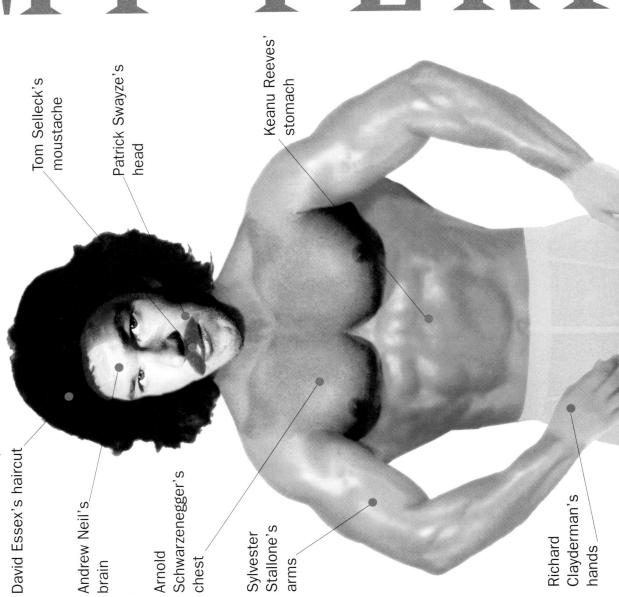

# MY PERF

Tom Selleck's moustache

Patrick Swayze's head

Keanu Reeves' stomach

David Essex's haircut

Andrew Neil's brain

Arnold Schwarzenegger's chest

Sylvester Stallone's arms

Richard Clayderman's hands

# ECT MAN

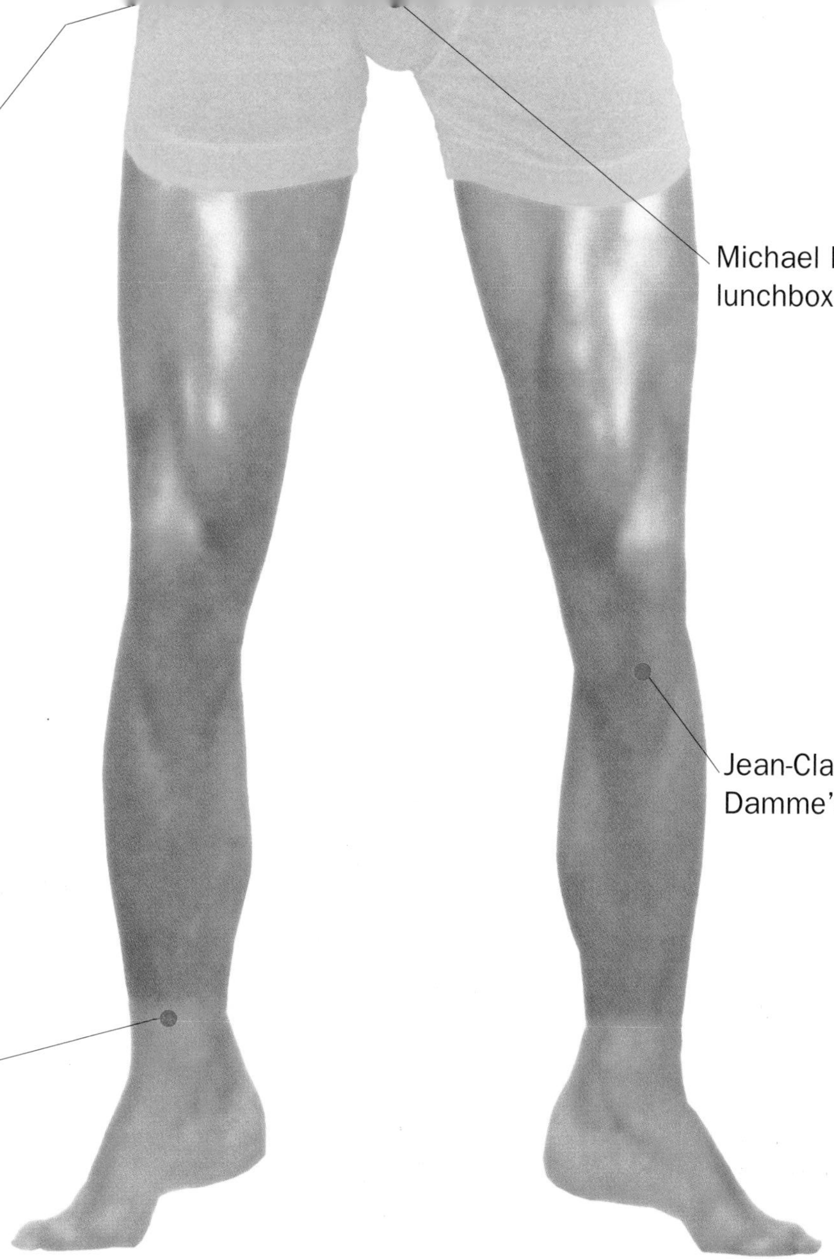

Michael Douglas' lunchbox

Jean-Claude Van Damme's legs

Kevin Costner's bum

Barry Sheene's feet

# FAT B⬤B'

PINK PYJAMA CASE IN THE SHAPE
OF A HIPPOPOTAMUS

**1**

BLANCMANGE

**2**

PINK MARSHMALLOWS IN A BOWL
BESIDE YOUR BED

**3**

FAT BOB NAKED

**4**

PINK DUVET AND MATCHING
PILLOWCASES

**5**

**42**

# Your Bedroom

CHERRY BLOSSOM PETALS

A TIN OF SPAM

**6**

**7**

LAURENT PERRIER PINK CHAMPAGNE

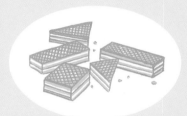

WAFER CREAMS
(AS SEEN IN TEA TIME ASSORTED)

**8**

**9**

ALBINO BUNNY RABBIT

**10**

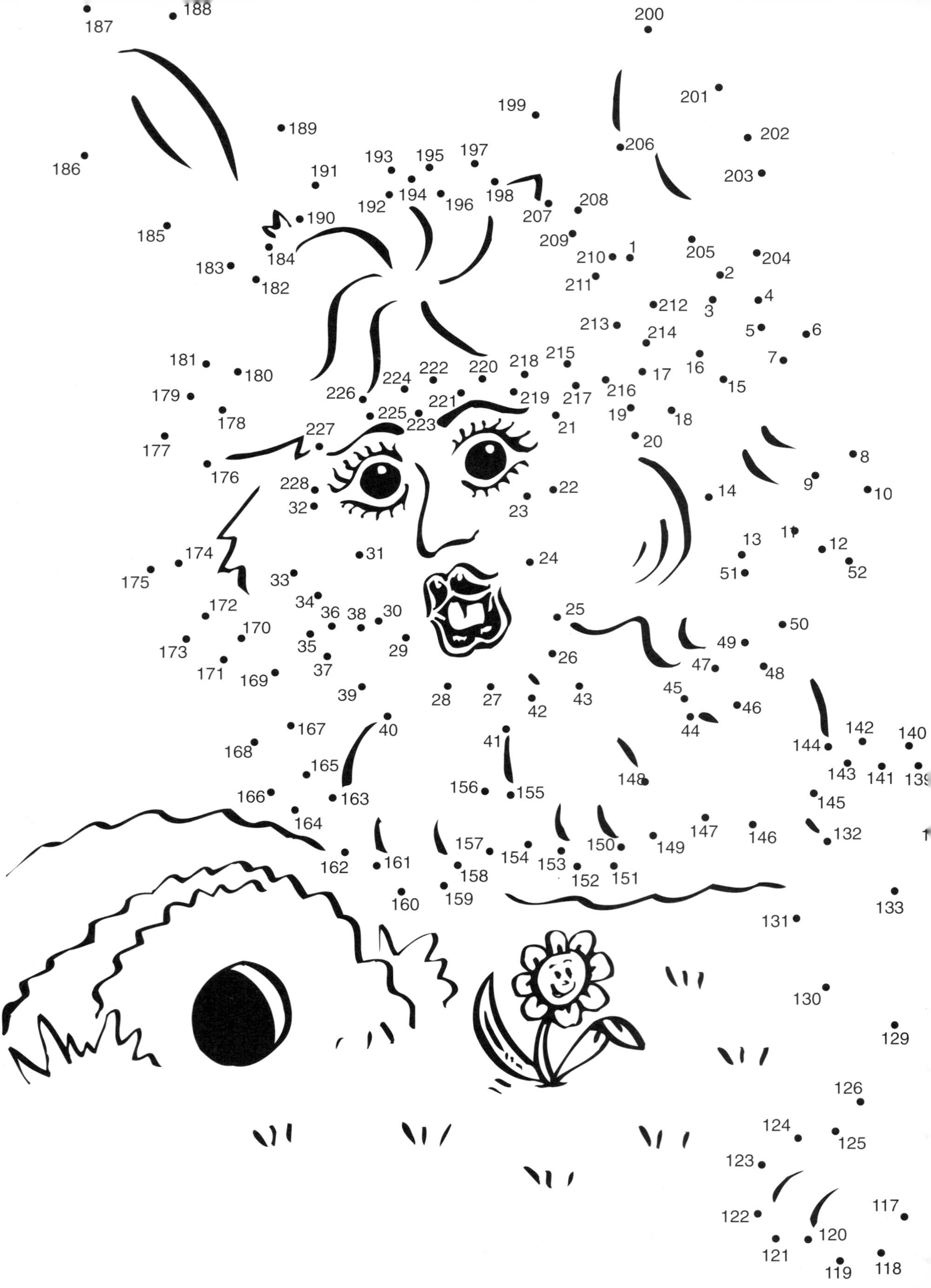

66
68
64
70
65 67
62 69 72
63 71
61 73
60 74
59 75
58 57 77 76
56
54 79
55 81 78
53 83 82 80

84

85

36

86

87

88 90
89

110
107
109 108
91
11 106
112 92
105
7
113
93
114 104
103
115
102
101 94
100
99 95
98 97 96

45

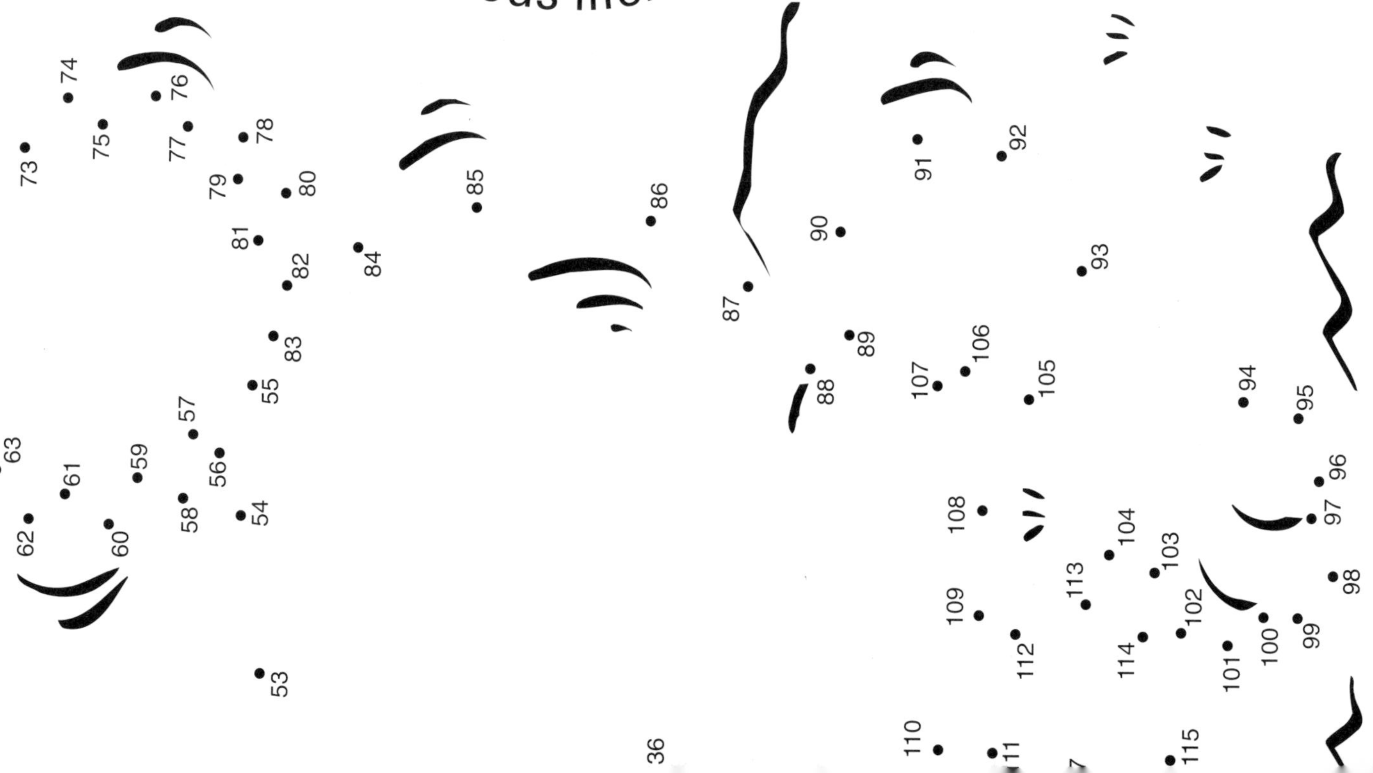

Well done Trish,
now you'll be 'beating them
off with a sh**ty stick'
thanks to lots of make-up.

# Pauline's Makeover

*It will come as a surprise to a lot of people that withou lots of make-up even I can look as rough as a bear's arse.*

People often stop me in the street and ask, 'Pauline you always seem to have a happy breezy smile on your face, even after a heavy night on the town. How do you achieve this?' The answer is simple. **LOTS OF MAKE-UP™!**

Two hours later. Voilà!
It's as simple as that.

# Reveal The Beauty Within

# DRESS PAULINE

## WHATEVER THE OCCASION PAULINE LOVES TO LOOK HER BEST.

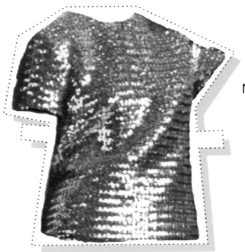

Now you have your very own Pauline to cut out and keep. Simply cut along the dotted line.

Then 'dress her' in the oufit of your choice. It's as simple as that!

Mix and match to your heart's content. The combinations are almost endless.

Or for the boys, if you're feeling a bit saucy, put on some music by Jon Bon Jovi and slowly peel off her clothes.

Why not glue the figure to some cardboard, attach strings and watch her dance to pop music?

Pretty Woman
KRAMER VERSUS KRAMER
Dirty Dancing
AN OFFICER AND A GENTLEMAN
GHOST
THE STUD
TOP GUN
DISCLOSURE
THE BODYGUARD
scrubbers

# These are a few of

1 BLACK LACE (NOT THE BAND)

2 FOUR-POSTER BEDS CARVED FROM IVORY

3 FROGGY'S FUN PUB, OLDHAM

*my favourite things*

♪ 4
HORSE-DRAWN
CARRIAGES

♪ 5
MAGNUM (THE SERIES
AND THE ICE CREAM

♪ 7
BROWN PAPER PACKAGES
TIED UP WITH STRING

♪ 6
TIRAMISU

♪ 8
ANDRE AGASSI'S BUM

♪ 9
ANTONIO
BANDERAS'S
BUM

♪ 10
FERRERO
ROCHER

55

# *These are a few things*

1 **BEARDS**

2 **SECOND-HAND FURNITURE**

3 **CAROL VORDERMAN**

4 **MEN WHO 'JUST WANT TO BE FRIENDS'**

5 **AIR PISTOLS**

6 **BBC 2**

7 **EGG-FRIED RICE**

# I can't bleedin' stand

**8** ♪ CAMPING TRIPS

**9** ♪ SMALL TELLIES

**10** ♪ YASMIN LE BON

# PAULINE'S
## GAME FOR ANYTHING

You read an article in which Patrick Swayze mentions he likes big girls.

Your new home perm kit makes your hair go all frizzy. You have to stay in for the evening and watch *Kavanagh QC*.

All your lacey white underwear gets put in the wash with Paul's brown pants. Everything turns beige.

**24** Move forward one space

20

19

18

**14** Miss a turn

15

16

**17** Move back two spaces

Bella magazine arrives but the free sachet of Max Factor moisturiser is missing.

13

41

12

42

There's a new postman who looks a bit like Jean Claude Van Damme but with a bit of a pot belly.

**43** Move back one space

11

**9** Move forward one space

10

8

7

Your Anne Summers party is ruined when a drunken Paul walks in holding a vibrator pretending to be a Dalek.

44

45

1

2

3

5

**6** Miss a turn

4

## START

BT Personal Communications
Telecom Ho

5 W932 FF
6

NG ENQUIRIES
ON 0800 15011
PM

I'M A SEXY MOTHER

E.M.R PRESEN

## Chris de Burgh

£25

IN CONCERT

18 NOVEMBER 1997 8.39PM
AT M.U.F.C OLD TRAFFORD

STRETFORD END A24
TICKET NO.00025

STRETFORD END A24

TICKET NO.00025

## Remind

The bill we sent you do

If you have paid recentl

However, if you have n
using the attached slip b

PLEASE NOTE.

THERE I

OU WILL BE PAYING OR

TAN TASTIC

SOLARIUM

**SPECIAL OFFER**
## HALF PRICE
ANNUAL MEMBERSHIP

BRING THIS COUPON TO:
TAN TASTIC, 12 GORTON
ROAD, OPPOSITE THE
CREMATORIUM

overdue  £723.60

It's very peaceful here.
The whole area is
unspoilt. The scenery
is just hills and trees
as far as the eye can
see. It's one of the few
places left untouched
by tourism. The only
sound is the summer breeze
and the waves, lapping
against the sand. <u>I CAN'T
BLEEDING STAND IT</u>. I'm
coming home. Paul.
Love to Peculiar ✗✗

Over: view of Portmadog by night

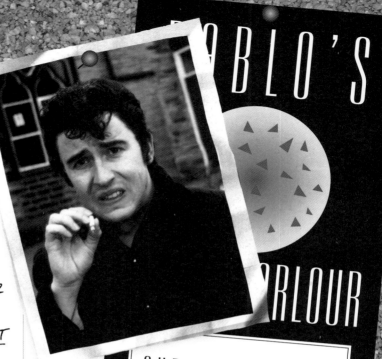

# PABLO'S

# PARLOUR

## OUR SPECIALITIES

### HAWAIIAN-5-O
HAM, MUSHROOMS, PINEAPPLE,
COCONUT, CHEESE

### MEXICAN HOT
GROUND BEEF, RED PEPPERS,
CHILLI, TOMATOES, MOZZARELLA

### SEAFOOD SAU̶
ANCHOVI̶

unsuccessful and I'm afraid we are unable to of̶
interview for the position of air hostess at this
Best wishes for your future career.

Yours sincerely

*Clare Fraser*

Clare Fraser
Human Resources Manager

**BRITISH AIRWAYS** ✈

- Take leather basque to dry cleaners
- Shampoo bedroom carpet
- Pick up Bob's anti-depressants
- Set video for 'Soldier Soldier'
- Pick up family allowance
- 3 o'clock - hairdressers.

# PLAYBIRD OF THE MONTH

# PAULINE

## AS YOU'VE NEVER SEEN HER BEFORE

GIRLS' TALK
# 0004 BROTHERS
PAUL IS CHANGING. HE'S DECIDED TO GET FIT.
SPORTS CENTRE
TENNIS
FITNESS GYM

# Dear Pauline

## HE WANTS US TO HAVE SEX

*Dear Aunty Pauline,*

**My boyfriend David is a six foot two fireman who looks a bit like Antonio Banderos. He says he loves me more than anything in the world. We have been going together for some time. The thing is he wants us to have sex but I'm not sure as I am still a virgin. What should I do?**

*Shiobhan, Cheetham Hill*

**Dear Shiobhan,**

Have a full structural survey by an experienced professional done before you invest in his property. I provide such a service at very competitive rates. In this instance it would be on the house. ■

## IT STILL HURTS

*Dear Aunty Pauline,*

**I've got thrush. What should I do?**

*Brenda Gilhaley*

**Dear Brenda,**

Use Canesten. ■

# Star Letter

## CENTRE OF ATTENTION

*Dear Pauline,*

**I have very large breasts. No matter how I try to hide this fact, in any gathering, my breasts always seem to become the centre of attention. People point, stare, snigger, and raise their eye-brows. Can you give me any advice?**

*Caroline, Didsbury*

**Dear Caroline,**

Spoilt for choice. Bleach your hair, wear short skirts and high heels. Let them know it doesn't bother you by being loud and giggling a lot. ■

## I HEAR THEM LAUGHING

*Dear Aunty Pauline,*

**I have been best friends with Elaine for six years now. Recently I started going out with a new boyfriend, Todd. Now Elaine turns up unannounced at my house but only when Todd is there. When I leave the room I can hear them giggling together and when I return they look sheepish and guilty. I fear I'm going to lose both the man I love and my best friend.**

*Jannine, Stoke*

**Dear Jannine,**

Find a quiet moment with Elaine. Sit her down and take both her hands in yours. Tell her that boyfriends come and go but real friendship lasts forever. Say that you understand her attraction to Todd but that she must understand that Todd is your boyfriend and if she so much as looks at him again she'll be controlling a wheelchair through a straw. ■

66

## I WANT TO LEAVE MY JOB

*Dear Aunty Pauline,*

**I work next to a building site. When I choose to wear something that is slightly revealing the workmen wolf whistle, make rude gestures and shout things like 'show us your tits'. When I get to the office my colleagues, who are predominantly male make suggestive remarks and constant sexual innuendos throughout the day. Some even slap and pinch my bottom as I walk past. When I talk to my boss he simply stares at my chest and makes panting noises like a dog. He always brushes against me when we pass in the corridor. What can I do?**

*Sophie Carter, Peterborough*

### Dear Sophie,

I don't quite understand what your problem is. This is a page for people with problems and it really doesn't help matters when people like you write these insensitive letters which appear to be nothing more than an excuse for bragging. ■

## FUNNY HABITS

*Dear Aunty Pauline,*

**Every time I eat, I want to have sex. What can I do?**

*Sabrina, Penzance*

### Dear Sabrina,

Tuck in. ■

## CAN'T CHOOSE

*Dear Aunty Pauline,*

**I've recently been seeing a guy called Martin who I met in a local pub three weeks ago. We've been out on a couple of dates and I was really getting to like him until the night I met his brother, Spike, who was working backstage at a David Copperfield concert. When our eyes met it really was like magic! Now I'm so confused. I can't choose between Martin and Spike. What can I do?**

*Cleo Dawson, Matlock*

### Dear Cleo,

I understand exactly what you must be going through. I had a similar experience a few years ago with two brothers who owned a minicab. One used to drive days, the other would drive nights. The important thing is to keep a cool head and to make a clear decision. I made the very clear decision to shag them both. ■

## HE SAYS HE LOVES ME

*Dear Aunty Pauline,*

**I love my boyfriend very much and we have a deep and fulfilling relationship in many ways. However, when we sleep together he finds it very difficult to become aroused due to a deep rooted psychological fear of rejection. What should I do?**

*Rosemary Cliff, Dundee*

### Dear Rosemary,

Dump him. ■

## I'M VERY CONFUSED

*Dear Aunty Pauline,*

**I'm very concerned about my sexuality. Recently I've found myself attracted to women. I think I may have bi-sexual or lesbian tendencies. As my new-found yearning builds with each passing day I feel the act of lesbian congress is inevitable. As this is uncharted territory I have great feelings of trepidation. I know that it would greatly ease my anxiety if you were to describe in graphic detail a typical lesbian sexual encounter. Proper girl-on-girl action, you know, 69'ers and stuff. The full monty.**

*Uma Pfeiffer, North Manchester*

### Dear Paul,

If you want to stimulate yourself sexually with pseudo-lesbian erotica there are plenty of opportunities. Simply look in the classified section of any of the pornographic magazines that you keep hidden behind the hot water tank. ■

*Pauline Calf*

67

*1* You've just seen the film 'The Piano' and in the heated post-film discussion you are asked to comment on the performance of Harvey Keitel.

### DO YOU SAY ?

❑ For me, Keitel will always be quintessentially linked with Scorcese. [1]

❑ Keitel displayed profound sensitivity unseen in his previous work. [3]

❑ He's a bit tubby, but he's got a nice arse. [6]

*2* You have just bought yourself a brand new Ford Fiesta Finesse and your friend asks you what you like about the car.

### DO YOU RESPOND ?

❑ The overall fuel economy linked to its day-to-day running costs and practicality. [1]

❑ The responsive performance and predictable front wheel drive handling. [3]

❑ It's turquoise. [6]

*3* A man in a dirty mac flashes you in the park.

### DO YOU ?

❑ Burst into tears and run screaming for help. [1]

❑ Assert yourself by confronting the perpetrator and stating that you refuse to be intimidated by an inadequate display of remedial sexuality. [3]

❑ Kick him in the balls and keep kicking until he bursts into tears and runs off screaming. [6]

*4* You're at the Debenhams January sale. An item catches your eye but as you grasp one end of the garment you realise another woman already has hold of the other end.

### DO YOU ?

❑ Release your grip and apologise immediately, before smiling and wishing her a Happy New Year. [1]

❑ Throw yourself on her mercy explaining it's something you've set your heart on since you first saw it in the shop last September. [3]

❑ Pull the garment until it tears in two, whilst saying, 'It wouldn't fit you anyway, you fat cow.' [6]

*5* You are stopped by a policeman for speeding.

### DO YOU ?

❑ Accept the solemn rebuke and pay an on-the-spot fine. [1]

❑ Argue your case by pointing out the number of other drivers passing at the same speed. [3]

❑ Shove his face in your cleavage and your hand in his pants and hold on tight until his protestations turn to cries of, 'Oh no, not again', 'for God's sake hurry up' and 'I'll let you off with a caution.' [6]

# PAULINE?

**6** You're at a nightclub and are accused of trying to cop off with Tina Beasley's fiancé, Carl from Do It All.

❏ I'm already in a trusting and fulfilling relationship. [1]

❏ Although Carl is a powerful and handsome man I realise that no one could love him the way you do and all I want is for you two to have a long and happy marriage together. [3]

❏ I've had him. [6]

**7** You are at Stringfellows nightclub, standing innocently at the bar, when you are approached by a fat, ugly middle-aged man wearing a gold Rolex watch, who smiles and offers to buy you a drink.

### DO YOU ?

❏ Decline politely and explain that you are waiting for your friend. [1]

❏ Accept his offer with an open mind. Try not to judge him by his appearance. Avoid the clichés, raise yourselves above the vulgar throng and talk honestly to one another. [3]

❏ Get him to keep you and your friends in 'Taboo and Black' all night long whilst giggling like a school girl, flirting outrageously by mussing his hair and calling him your little teddy bear. Bid him goodnight with a peck on the cheek and ask to see him again. Over the next few week he takes you to the swankiest restaurants in town. You dangle the promise without ever quite delivering sexual gratification. Eventually, when he goes down on his knees, saying he can't control his libido any longer, you burst into tears, saying you need solid proof of his love before you can let him take your virginity. Wait until he has spent at least a grand on jewellery before telling him you don't think you're right for each other and dumping him like a ton of hot bricks. Pawn half the jewellery and book a holiday for you and your mates with Club Med. [6]

# Instant Pauline

Cut along dotted line.
Tie string in holes at side.
Wear something shiny.

# Instant Petula

Cut along dotted line. Tie string in holes at side. Gurgle.

# Instant Fat Bob

Cut along dotted line.
Tie string in holes at side. Mope.

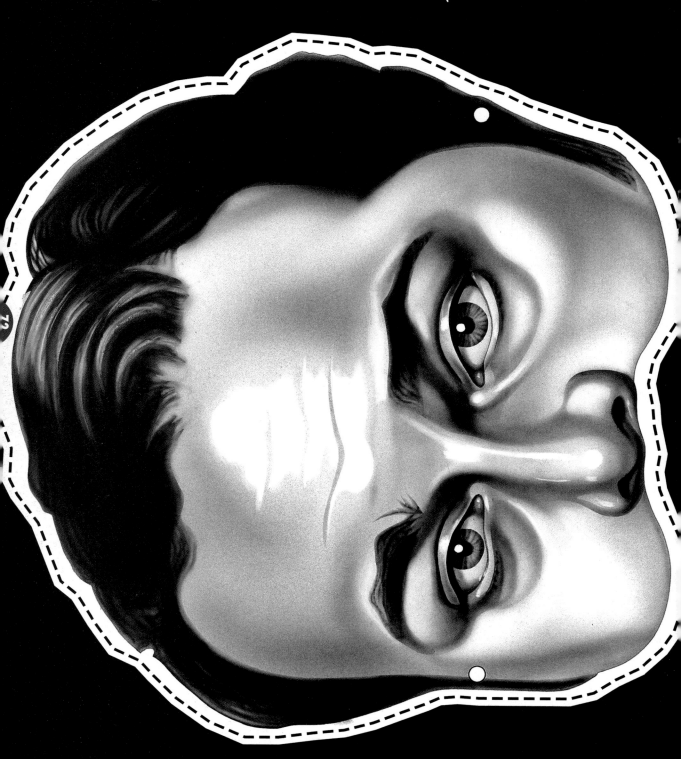

# Paul's Book for Boys

# Paul's Book for Boys

STEVE COOGAN AND HENRY NORMAL

Hodder & Stoughton

First published in Great Britain in 1996 by Hodder and Stoughton
A division of Hodder Headline PLC

10  9  8  7  6  5  4  3  2  1

British Library Cataloguing in Publication Data
A CIP catalogue record for this title is available from the British Library

ISBN   0 340 68066 0

**Design and artwork** by THE BRIDGEWATER BOOK COMPANY
**Designers:** Peter Bridgewater and John Christopher
**Illustration:** Paul Allen, Paul Collicut, Ivan Hissey, Kurt Hoyte,
Mainline Design, Fred Pipes, and Curtis Tappenden
**Steve Coogan's wardrobe by** Marcia Stanton
**Steve Coogan's make-up and styling by** Lisa Cavalli-Green

GRATEFUL ACKNOWLEDGMENTS TO:

Geoff Posner, Dave Tyler, John Thompson, Patrick Marber, Sandra Gough, Sally Rogers,
Lisa Cavalli-Green, Marcia Stanton, John Wood, Jan Murphy, Angela Pell, John Hannah

Printed and bound in Great Britain by
Butler & Tanner Ltd, Frome and London

Hodder and Stoughton
A division of Hodder Headline PLC
338 Euston Road
London NW1 3BH

DEDICATED TO

# David Hasslehoff

YOU LUCKY BASTARD

# Contents

And don't miss The Paul and Pauline Calf Audio Experience – with Fat Bob and lots of extra material – available now from Hodder Headline Audiobooks on cassette and CD.

Steve Coogan & Henry Normal

**Paul's**

THINGS YOU SHOULDN'T SAY TO YOUR GIRLFRIEND'S FATHER
The art of seduction

CD for BOYS

Are You Paul

# SCHOOL REPORT

## Paul Calf     AGE 15     CLASS 4b

### ENGLISH

Made some progress when I pointed out that 'Bag
of shite' was an expressive colloquial metaphor.

*H. Townley*
*60/100*

### ENGLISH LITERATURE

Paul has embraced the Greek Philosophers
this year. He has even suggested a field
trip to Corfu.

(A)
*Mr Knight*

### MATHEMATICS

His ability to visualise any problem in the guise
of betting slips has helped him tremendously.

*Ms Brown*
(C)

### GEOGRAPHY

Couldn't find his arse with
both hands.

*JJones*
*30/100*

### SOCIAL SCIENCE

Paul's project on ~~PHILLIPENO~~ Philipino brides is one of
the most extensive and thoroughly researched pieces I
have ever come across.

*Mrs Stanley*
(A)

### HISTORY

Paul thinks that the dark ages were
during the miners' strike 1973-74.

*R8* (E)

### BIOLOGY

Very keen. Gave a very comprehensive explanation of the
reproduction process, although this would have benefited
from less frequent use of the word 'Spunk'.

*JSmith* (E)

| | |
|---|---|
| **PHYSICS**<br><br>This boy has never attended any of my classes, yet his mark matches exactly that of the brightest boy in the class. | P. Corrigan<br>(A) |
| **CHEMISTRY**<br><br>Paul ~~CALF~~ Calf is shit at Chemistry and I hate him. | Mr Cragg<br>(E) |
| **METAL WORK**<br><br>Shows great aptitude. Paul will have a promising career as a locksmith. | A.A Smith<br>(D) |
| **P.E**<br><br>For a striker, Paul spends too much time in his own penalty area chatting with the goalkeeper, ~~FAT~~ Bob Boyle. | R Roberts<br>20/100 |
| **CLUBS AND SOCIETIES**<br>Chairman of the video-lending club.<br>Photographic society (banned). | H.H (D) |
| **FORM TEACHER**<br><br>Shows great initiative. When a fire started in the Chemistry lab, Paul was first at the scene. He managed to stop the fire spreading beyond Mr Cragge's office. | B. Richards<br>(D) |
| **HEADMASTER**<br><br>Despite encouraging signs of Paul's apparent progress in certain areas, I feel it my duty to point out that Paul is regarded by staff and pupils alike as something of a twat. | PB (40) |

ANYWAY, IT WAS BLACK AND WHITE WITH **SUBTITLES**.

IT WAS ABOUT **PEASANTS** OR SOMETHING.

I CAME OUT AFTERWARDS AND CORNERED THIS **STUDENT**.

WHAT DO YOU **RECKON** TO THAT?

HE SAID,

I WAS MOVED BY THE **IRONIC JUXTAPOSITION** OF REALISM AND SYMBOLISM.

IT WAS **A BAG O' SHITE**. HAVE YOU SEEN TERMINATOR 2?

PAUL'S DESERT ISLAND DISCS

EYE OF THE TIGER

COMPACT
disc
DIGITAL AUDIO

SURVIVOR

1

KUNG FU
FIGHTING

陰 陽

COMPACT
disc
DIGITAL AUDIO

CARL DOUGLAS

2

Into the
valley

The Skids

3

**Heil Hitler**

*Hello or Goodbye (depending on the circumstances). Also an ironic put down.*

**Nein Herr Commandant**

*No, Mr Commandant.*

**Schnell, Schnell**

*Fast!, Fast!*

**Kommen Sie hier bitte**

*Come here (you look a little suspicious).*

**Das Vaterland**

*The Fatherland.*

**Achtung, Achtung**

*Attention, Attention.*

**Where are your papers, Fräulein?**

*Where are your papers, woman (you've been rumbled).*

**Himmel!**

*Oh dear!*

**Ahhhhhh!**

*Ahhhhh!*

# DAILY ECHO CALF

**❝ ... I was up in court last week for ABH, Actual Bodily Harm, not grievous, I'm not an animal. I conducted my own defence and I said... ❞**

"Ladies and gentlemen of the jury, I am not on trial here today, society is on trial, the whole judicial system is on trial. Oh f*** it, I'm on trial, aren't I? But I'm not in contention with the prosecution's version of events. On that we agree. There was a student, he was acting up, he got a slap. But I was under severe provocation. There I was, having a quiet pint, when a student walked past and nudged me, causing me to spill a bit. I did what any fine, upstanding citizen would do. I followed him to the toilet and kicked his head in. Perhaps I was a little overzealous. Perhaps I should have stopped kicking him when he was in the ambulance. But I did what I did because I want to live in a world where we can have a pint without fear of being nudged by a student. Is that a crime? Is it a crime to want to live in a world of peace and harmony? Is it a crime to live in a world of love? Is it a crime to hit a student across the back of the head with a snooker ball in a sock?"

**That's where the defence's case collapsed.**

# N COURT

14 — A Scandinavian cartoon season on Channel 4

Nick Berry in 'Heartbeat'

15 — Bob Hoskins doing BT adverts

12 — Shandy

11 — Posh birds with studs in their noses

13 — 'Eastenders' when Nick Berry was in it

15 — Costume dramas

19 — That bald twat who used to do 'The Crystal Maze'

17 — Programmes on Channel 4 where they shake the camera around a lot

6 — Hairdressers in jeeps

# THE BAG O'SHITE TOP 20

**18** Male models

**17** The chart-topping hit 'Every Loser Wins' performed by Nick Berry

**20** People who hang rugs and musical instruments on the wall

**19** Camden market

**15** Posh blokes who make out that they're not posh

**16** National Express coaches

**6** Goatee beards

**9** Cuban hats

**13** 'Ballykissangel'

**14** Snowboarding

# BANGED UP!

When the judge passed sentence I said nothing. I stared him out. He bottled it and looked down at his notes. It was a victory of sorts. I wondered who looked more tragic – me in a Burton's suit handcuffed to a prison officer or his lordship wearing a long black dress and a wig like a girl. I think he knew. I smirked and swaggered as I was led away. I could almost hear the public gallery, 'There goes Calf, cool as a cucumber, down but not out'.

In the slammer no one asked what your crime was. We were all criminals. Who cared whether you'd murdered men? Whether you'd come a cropper on an armed robbery? Whether you'd masterminded gangland extortion or whether you'd been charged with 'Non-payment of a fine for non-payment of a TV licence fee'?

We were all in it together, doing bird, doing porridge, doing a stretch, serving a prison sentence, call it what you will. The language came easy to me. I was steeped in the folklore.

Then there were the screws. They were prisoners just the same as us, except they went home in the evenings. Occasionally there'd be a beating but no one laid a finger on you if you were a personal friend of Mr Big (like I was).

I became obsessed with escape. I stole a dessert spoon from the canteen and started to scrape away the plaster from the wall of my cell. I was careful to cover up the evidence of my progress with a topless picture of Linda Lusardi. God how she helped me through those nights. Thank you Linda. You are 'all-woman', except for my mum and my sister of course. I worked out that by scraping four hours a night within six years I could dig a tunnel to Freedom. At times it all semed so futile. My release date was five weeks away and I'd only been in there just over a fortnight.

Already I'd become institutionalised. Brutalised by an uncaring system.

When I left, I'd leave with a scar … I'd be a different man … a hard man.

Jimmy Boyle, John McVicar, The Krays, Paul Calf …. Just names to some people but this is their story as well as mine.

What lay outside for a marked man … unemployment, rejection, oblivion? I'd probably end up like the rest of them – a publishing deal, a guest spot on Pebble Mill, part of a penal reform pressure group on Kilroy and perhaps a guest columnist in the *Independent*.

Worse still, a one-man show at the Edinburgh festival.

# Chapter five

# BETRAYAL

I saw the Governor only once. He looked like Charlton Heston but fatter, with the voice of Larry Grayson. He was not a man to be crossed.

He told me there were two ways of doing time, the easy way or the hard way. I told him I preferred the easy way but I was bluffing. I can't remember whose suggestion it was but there was a deal laid out that involved one of us grassing. In the end I let him believe I was going along with him, and the truth was I was going along with him but only I knew that for sure. I had the upper hand.

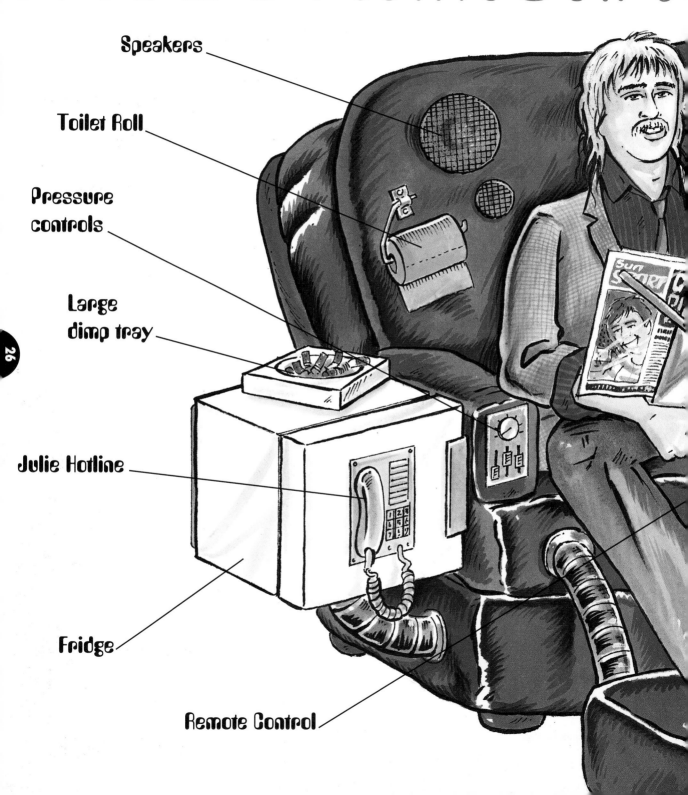

Speakers

Toilet Roll

Pressure controls

Large dimp tray

Julie Hotline

Fridge

Remote Control

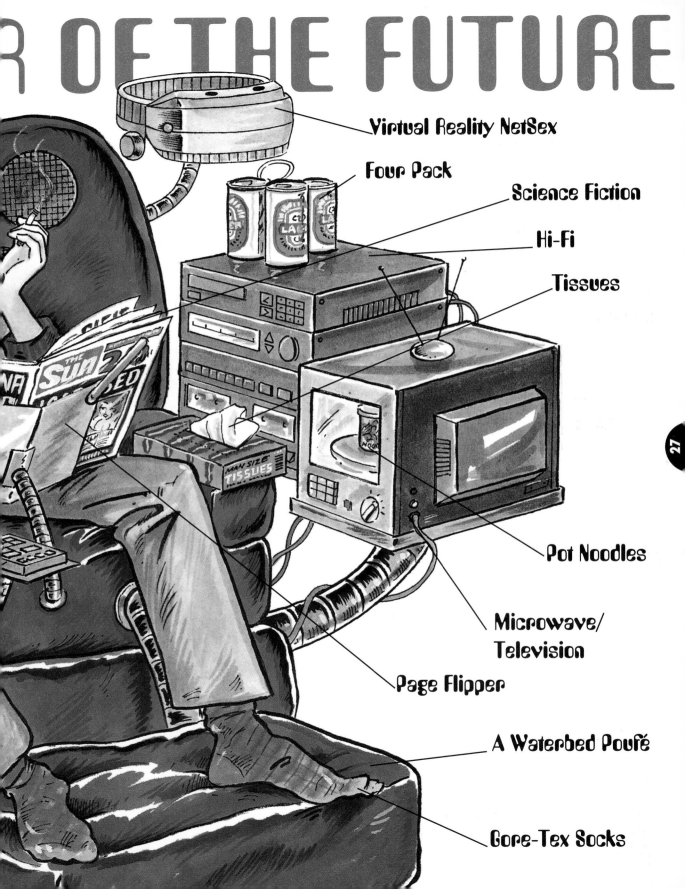

Virtual Reality NetSex

Four Pack

Science Fiction

Hi-Fi

Tissues

Pot Noodles

Microwave/
Television

Page Flipper

A Waterbed Poufé

Gore-Tex Socks

UNBEKNOWNST TO ME, A STUDENT HAPPENED TO BE RIDING BY ON HIS BIKE...

HUUK

AND I JUST HAPPENED TO **PUKE** IN THE BASKET ON THE FRONT THAT'S LIKE A TEA-STRAINER.

HE GOT OFF AND SAID,

ARGH!

YOU'VE RUINED MY NOTES ON THE SOCIAL IMPLICATIONS OF **DEPRIVATION** ON THE URBAN MALE.

I SAID, 'DO YOU KNOW WHAT YOU CAN DO WITH YOUR NOTES? DO YOU KNOW WHERE YOU CAN STICK 'EM? IN YOUR SADDLE-BAG - IT'S WATER-PROOF'.

COURSE I DIDN'T! I SAID,

STICK 'EM UP YOUR ARSE, YOU **BAG O' SHITE.**

# Paul Calf

## Man Of ~~Letters~~

**REF:** NA 23 56 93 XF/ 364 PC

Dear Mr Calf,

Having checked our records we can find no trace of the two dependants claimed on your recent application for supplementary benefit, Mr Pablo Calf and Mr Pedro Calf. We will require further details before your claim can be processed.

*R. Boyse*

Mr Richard Boyse
Assistant Claims Officer

Department of Social Security
NEWCASTLE UPON TYNE
NE98 1YX

---

Dear Mr Boyse,

Thank you for your letter of the 15th Aug. Although Pablo and Pedro were distressed at what they see as an intrusion into their private lives, I explained to them that Mr Boyse was an honest and decent man and that once he knew the full details of their tragic situation he would personally cut through the bureaucracy and send us the money rightfully due, to put a little food in their tummies. Here are the indisputable facts.

Pablo and Petro (twins, age 4) arrived in this country earlier last year. Not wanting to beat about the bush they are two little Spanish bastards, the result of a romantic liaison with a Catalonian flamenco dancer (~~Carmen Picasso~~) I met on Valentine's Day on a whistle-stop tour of North Manchester working men's clubs. The sound of castonets still brings a tear to my eye. Pablo and Petro now live with me following their mother's untimely death at the hands of a cruel matador, a bit like Antonio Banderas with an eyepatch and a bad knee. He wasn't very successful and took it out on the women! I hope this is sufficient detail for your records.

If we backdate the benefit to, say, last Christmas it's £2250. I know how hard pressed your resoures are so let's say £2000.

P.S. Due to a problem with my bank which is proving less than co-operative at the moment, could you make the cheque payable to Moston Car Mart?

Paul

**REF:** NA 23 56 93 XF/ 364 PC

Dear Mr Calf,

Further to yours of the 17th instance, we note your comments. Regarding your 'facts' we would ask for some clarification. You claim the twins are four years' old and the relationship took place on Valentine's day which would thus be 14th Feb. 1992. According to our records, at this time you were serving two months in Stockton Prison for assaulting a police officer. We would like to know how it was possible to conduct this relationship whilst being detained at her Majesty's pleasure? Whilst writing we must point out that smokers' cough does not entitle you to a disablity allowance.

*R. Boyse .*

Mr Richard Boyse
Assistant Claims Officer

---

Dear Mr ~~Boyse~~ Boyse,
   Well done for spotting this glaring error. It appears we have both been the victim of an elaborate hoax by the murdering one-eyed matador who, on closer inspection, looks more like a fat Englebert Humperdink. It sickens me how ~~some~~ people attempt to defraud the laudable benefit system of this fine country.
   With regards to the disabil-ity allowance, it pains me to report that following a bout of excessive coughing, I've suf-fered a schism in my coccyx. I enclose a letter from my doctor confirming the extent of my ail-ment.

~~Paul Calf~~

---

Doctor Robert Boyle
General Practicianer

*NOT JUST CLUTCHES*

It is my concidered and learned opinion that Mr Calf should not undertake any work, what with his bad back and all. He has Schizoid Coccyx which I have found to be very painful under cross examina-tion.

Yours authoritatively

Doctor Bob

**REF:** NA 23 56 93 XF/ 364 PC

Dear Mr Calf,

We would draw your attention to the enclosed photographs taken earlier this week and, in view of the contents of same, ask if you wish to reconsider your claim for disability benefit.

As you are eligible for work please supply details of your efforts to obtain employment over the recent six-month period. Failure to provide information may result in withdrawal of benefit.

*R. Boyse*

Mr Richard Boyse
Assistant Claims Officer

INLAND REVENUE
PRIVATE
V. 124 P (PPI) (NEW)

ROYAL MAIL
POSTAGE PAID
GREAT BRITAIN
HQ 145

Dear Mr Boyse,

It fills me with despair that an hitherto honourable institution, such as the DSS, employs big brother tactics which twist and distort the truth to present an ugly picture, which is a complete travesty. The pictures in question may look to those with sick minds like an able-bodied Paul Calf loading boxes of dodgy electric equipment onto the back of a lorry, to line a wallet already bulging from fraudulently obtained government subsidy. But for those who care about truth it is clear these pictures show me voluntarily helping out the Meals on Wheels people during a brief but short-lived success in self-hypnotherapy, temporarily enabling me to overcome the agony of my affliction.

Since these pictures the severity of my pain seems to have regressed to my previous state. There are short but sporadic periods when I am able to walk. As a rule I find I can achieve some mobility between the hours of seven thirty to eleven pm Mon to Sat, eight o'clock to ten thirty Sunday. I look forward to receiving my claim in full.

On an entirely unconnected and separate matter, let me say how sorry I am to hear that you recently had all your wheels stolen from your Ford Fiesta 1.1L including, I think I'm right in saying, the spare which I'm reliably informed was flat, which is of course, illegal. As luck would have it, I do know of a similar set which I can guarantee will fit perfectly. Perhaps we could come to some arrangement.

I applied for the following
vacancies.
Head of Current Affairs BBC
World Service
No reply
Greater Manchester Police Force
Interviewed and cautioned over
an unrelated matter
Senior Lecturer in Sociology
Liverpool Metropolitan Univerity
(formerly Liverpool Poly) -
shortlisted
Market Reseach Consultant for
the following companies:
Heineken
Kestrel
Carling Black Label
Hoffmeister
McEwans Export
Labatts

PAUL

**REF:** NA 23 56 93 XF/ 364 PC

Dear Mr Calf,

I am pleased to inform you that having reviewed
the situation in the light of recent
developments, your claim is to be met in full.
There seems to have been some confusion on
our part.

*R. Boyse.*

Mr Richard Boyse
Assistant Claims Officer

P.S Thank you for the 'new' wheels. I was
doubly impressed as it appears on the receipt that
they were fitted by your doctor.

Receipt no.
Date    /  /

↑

NOT JUST CLUTCHES

Mr Boyse

Ford Fiesta 1.1i wheels

5 @ £50

£250

Received with thanks
Bob Boyle

# Dress Paul

Dress Paul in the Man City kit and be amazed how he looks a bit like Dennis Law (with a moustache).

Dress Paul in the leopard skin underpants. Voilà! Rod Stewart (with a moustache).

If you're feeling adventurous make your own clothes. It's not poofy.

How many celebrities can you make him look a bit like?

35

# THE WORLD 25p
## According To CALF

### #0005 BEREAVEMENT

I HAD SOME BAD NEWS THE OTHER DAY. MY DAD DIED. HE HAD A HEART ATTACK WATCHING BAYWATCH. IT'S WHAT HE WOULD HAVE WANTED.

BUT WHEN HE WAS ALIVE, I USED TO LOOK AT HIM AND THINK, **YOU SAD PISSED-UP OLD F\*\*\*ER**. YOU KNOW, THERE BUT FOR THE GRACE OF GOD.

BUT I OFTEN THINK OF HIM UP THERE, IN **THE EVER LASTING PUB IN THE SKY** WHERE THEY NEVER CALL TIME. LAUGHING, SINGING, DANCING, PLAYING DARTS WITH ST PETER, GOOSING THE ANGELS, DOING HIS ELVIS IMPRESSION – TO ELVIS. GETTING ON EVERYONE'S TITS AS USUAL.

## The Ascent of Calf

Mollusc

Amphibian

Tree Shrew

Ape

Australopithecus robustus

I'VE BEEN LISTENING TO THE RADIO A LOT RECENTLY, COS THE RADIO HELPS YOU COME TO TERMS WITH BAD NEWS. COS THEY HAVE THE NEWS EVERY HOUR.

LIKE YOU MIGHT HEAR ON THE **ELEVEN O'CLOCK** NEWS SOME BLOKE'S BEEN MURDERED.

THEN IT'S **TWELVE O'CLOCK**, SOME BLOKE'S BEEN MURDERED.

**ONE O'CLOCK**, SOME BLOKE'S BEEN MURDERED. EVERY HOUR SOME BLOKE'S BEEN MURDERED.

BY DINNER TIME THE NEXT DAY YOU THINK, **OH F*** HIM!** I DIDN'T DO IT. IT'S NOT MY FAULT. D'YOU KNOW WHAT I MEAN?

Paul Calf

Homo erectus

Homo sapiens

# The team that should have been:

Substitute: Dennis Tueart

Goalkeeper Gordon Banks

Substitute: Gerd Muller

Manager Alf Ramsey

Substitute: Mike Summerbee

10
Pele

9
Paul Calf

2
Norman Hunter

7
Rodney Marsh

38

# Paul's fantasy football team

Substitute: Joe Corrigan

Substitute: Tommy Booth

**5** Johan Cruyff

**8** Uvay Rossler

**11** Dennis Law

**6** Colin Bell

**3** Franz Beckenbauer

**4** Francis Lee

39

| D | O | G | S | B | O | L | L | O | C | K | S |
|---|---|---|---|---|---|---|---|---|---|---|---|
| O | Y | B | H | A | R | P | L | A | G | E | R |
| G | J | C | A | G | P | A | S | E | X | S | P |
| S | I | U | G | O | L | M | A | M | O | T | I |
| H | F | A | G | S | K | E | Q | Z | A | R | D |
| E | B | W | I | H | A | A | A | N | A | E | M |
| A | K | A | N | I | T | R | O | C | I | L | A |
| D | N | S | G | T | Q | X | Z | I | A | L | R |
| J | U | L | I | E | A | U | B | T | P | A | S |
| Z | F | O | D | A | S | K | Y | T | V | G | B |
| W | R | I | N | H | R | W | A | R | S | E | A |
| T | O | G | Y | J | A | D | K | L | E | R | R |
| V | C | R | C | N | P | S | Y | T | I | T | S |

Find some of Paul's favourite things and phrases hidden in this word maze.

Join the dots to find out what Paul was in a previous life.

●5

●104

94●

95● ●103

93●

●102

●96

92●

●101

●76

75●

99● ●100

●77

91 ●90

9

●74

●89

78 ●79

●73

87● ●88

80● ●86

81 85

●84

82●

83

47

# PAUL'S TOP-TEN GIRLFRIENDS

*That he would like to have*

### SAM 1 FOX

YEAH, GOD DID BLESS HER AND SHE DID BLESS US APLENTY.

### JULIE 2

SHE IS A GODDESS IN MY EYES, BUT THE THOUGHT OF HER SHAG-GING TONY DOES MY HEAD IN AND PRECLUDES HER FROM THE NUMBER ONE SLOT.

### PAMELA 3 ANDERSON

SHE WON'T BE HEAD-HUNTED BY NASA, BUT THEN WHO WANTS TO SHAG BUZZ ALDRIN?

### LYNDA LUSARDI 4

AS A PAGE THREE STUNNER SHE BRIGHTENED UP MY BREAKFAST. I JUST WISHED SHE'D COOKED IT FOR ME.

### LIZ 5 HURLEY

TOP POSH BIRD. WITH LIZ ON MY ARM I WOULD BE GUARANTEED THE TOP TABLE AT ANY BEEFEATER.

## BIRD OFF THE RENAULT ADVERT 6

SPRITELY AND ELFIN-LIKE. 'AH PAUL'... 'AH NICOLE'... JE VEUX UN SNOG AVEC TOI DANS LE DERRIERE DE MA CORTINA.

## ZEINAB BADAWI 8

INTELLIGENT AND MYSTERIOUS. NO ONE KNOWS WHAT IT WOULD BE LIKE FOR HER TO TIE ME TO THE BED AND WHIP ME. IT REMAINS A MYSTERY.

## SHARON STONE 7

IN MY FANTASY NOT ONLY DOES SHE CROSS AND UNCROSS HER LEGS, BUT SHE BENDS DOWN TO PICK UP A 50P PIECE THAT I'VE GLUED TO THE FLOOR.

## DANII MINOGUE 9

LIKE KYLIE, BUT MORE FOR YOUR MONEY. I HAVE A RECURRING DREAM WHERE DANII IS GIVING ME A FOOT MASSAGE WHEN ('DING DONG') KYLIE ARRIVES TO BORROW A CUP OF SUGAR. THE REST IS ENJOYABLE BUT PREDICTABLE.

## BARMAID AT THE DOG'S HEAD 10

AVAILABLE.

43

45

# PAUL CALF'S THE

**6** A student falls off his bike. The feel-good factor puts a spring in your step. Move forward one space.

**7**

**8** Your mum makes you sausages in onion gravy. Move forward one space.

**9**

**10**

**11** You find a unopened Watneys party 7 yo hid in Fat Bob's garden in 1976. It has matured nicely Go forward 5 spaces.

**5**

**4**

**33** You bump into Raquel Welch and both fly off to Vegas to get married and live in a big house. Move forward eight spaces.

**32**

**34**

**3** The DSS has mistakenly sent you two giros. Move forward three spaces.

**35**

**31** You blag your way into a wedding reception and get pissed. Go to finish.

**30**

**36**

**2**

**37**

**start**

**38**

**1** BAG O' SHITE. Throw a six to start.

**41** It was all a dream. Go back to start.

**39**

**40**

**42**

# GAME OF LIFE

**15**
Someone tapes over your video of a very interesting documentary on prostitution in Thailand... Move back five spaces.

**16**

**17**

**18**
The off-licence has stopped selling Harp which means you have to fork out an extra 20p a can for Kestrel. This leaves you one can short. Miss a turn.

**19**

**20**

**21**

**22**

**23**

**24**

**12**

**13**

**14**

**27**
You wake and can't find your shoes. You have to walk home in your socks. Move back one space.

**26**

**25**
Fat Bob gets the use of Ford Zephyr for the weekend. You head for Prestatyn. Throw again.

**28**

**29**
Heartbeat gets a new series. Miss two turns.

**48**

**49**

**50**

**51**

**47**
You hear that City are relegated. Go back to start.

**44**
Get a lock-in at the student union bar. You're torn. Throw again.

**45**

**46**

**52**
THE DOG'S BOLLOCKS.

**finish**

**43**

AM I PISS

48

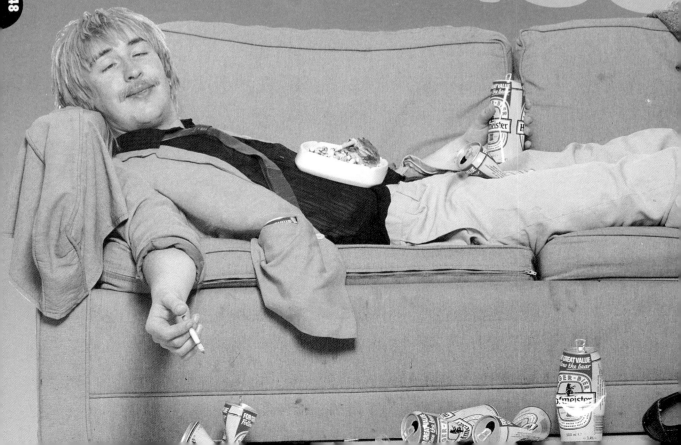

## Keep this list handy at all times

**1** Am I snogging someone who I don't know the name of?
yes/no

**2** Am I drinking Thunderbird from a plastic cup?
yes/no

**3** Am I leaning against the wall with one hand whilst being sick through my mouth and nose on the edge of a housing estate?
yes/no

**4** Am I talking very loudly two inches from someone's face?
yes/no

**5** Am I asleep on a bus at the terminus?
yes/no

**6** Am I brandishing a broken bottle and shouting at a bunch of squaddies 'c'mon you bunch of pansies'?
yes/no

**7** Am I pissing in my pants?
yes/no

**8** Can I hear someone banging on the door saying 'come on there's a queue out here'?
yes/no

**9** Am I talking enthusiastically with four strangers about setting up a business first thing tomorrow morning?
yes/no

**10** Am I using this paper to wipe my arse?
yes/no

# PAUL CALF'S
# GUIDE TO SELF
# DEFENCE

陰陽

# POTENTIAL INFLAMMATORY SITUATIONS

Having a quiet drink in a pub just outside Old Trafford whilst wearing a Man City scarf, and politely pointing out to a group of Man United supporters that their team would be a bunch of hairdressers if it wasn't for that garlic-chomping frog Cantona, wearing his collar up like that other twat Shaking Stevens. You would be surprised at the agressive and unwarranted behaviour that a little valid critism such as this can provoke. In this situation follow these simple guidelines:

## DO'S AND DON'TS

- ☑ Make sure you're standing near the exit
- ☑ Have a friend outside with the engine running (Fat Bob)
- ☑ Attempt to redirect their anger by mentioning Arsenal and in particular Ian Wright
- ☒ Go to the toilet
- ☒ Say 'I've had your sister and your mam and they were both crap'
- ☒ Bare your arse and say 'let's kiss and make up'

**IS SELF DEFENCE NECESSARY?**

If you were to ask me such a stupid question in public you would see just how necessary it is – you might as well say I'm soft, have a pop, it's on the house.

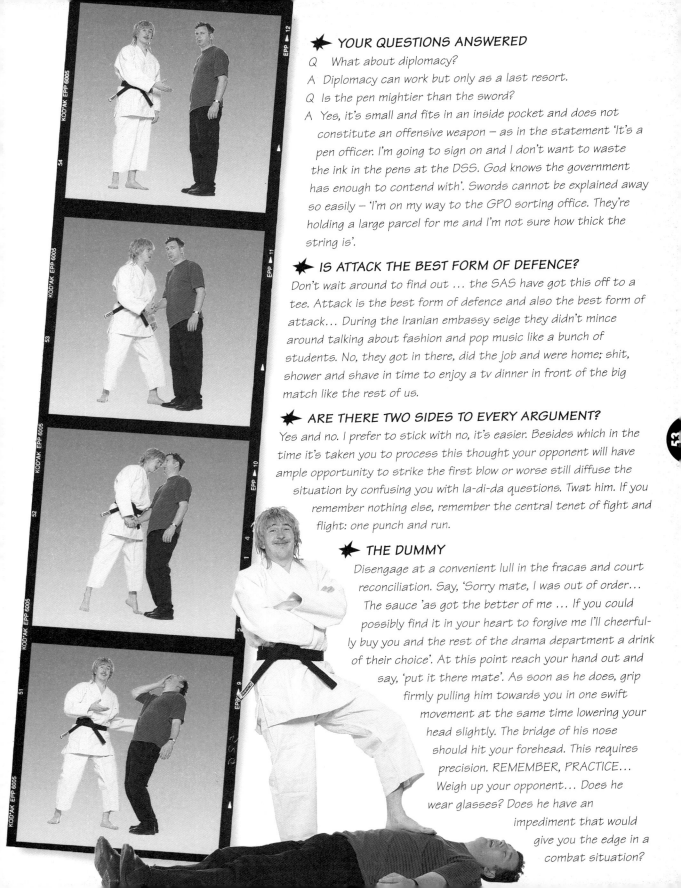

## ★ YOUR QUESTIONS ANSWERED

Q   What about diplomacy?

A   Diplomacy can work but only as a last resort.

Q   Is the pen mightier than the sword?

A   Yes, it's small and fits in an inside pocket and does not constitute an offensive weapon – as in the statement 'It's a pen officer. I'm going to sign on and I don't want to waste the ink in the pens at the DSS. God knows the government has enough to contend with'. Swords cannot be explained away so easily – 'I'm on my way to the GPO sorting office. They're holding a large parcel for me and I'm not sure how thick the string is'.

## ★ IS ATTACK THE BEST FORM OF DEFENCE?

Don't wait around to find out ... the SAS have got this off to a tee. Attack is the best form of defence and also the best form of attack... During the Iranian embassy seige they didn't mince around talking about fashion and pop music like a bunch of students. No, they got in there, did the job and were home; shit, shower and shave in time to enjoy a tv dinner in front of the big match like the rest of us.

## ★ ARE THERE TWO SIDES TO EVERY ARGUMENT?

Yes and no. I prefer to stick with no, it's easier. Besides which in the time it's taken you to process this thought your opponent will have ample opportunity to strike the first blow or worse still diffuse the situation by confusing you with la-di-da questions. Twat him. If you remember nothing else, remember the central tenet of fight and flight: one punch and run.

## ★ THE DUMMY

Disengage at a convenient lull in the fracas and court reconciliation. Say, 'Sorry mate, I was out of order... The sauce 'as got the better of me ... If you could possibly find it in your heart to forgive me I'll cheerfully buy you and the rest of the drama department a drink of their choice'. At this point reach your hand out and say, 'put it there mate'. As soon as he does, grip firmly pulling him towards you in one swift movement at the same time lowering your head slightly. The bridge of his nose should hit your forehead. This requires precision. REMEMBER, PRACTICE... Weigh up your opponent... Does he wear glasses? Does he have an impediment that would give you the edge in a combat situation?

# PAUL'S GUIDE TO SEDUC

**1** Don't be cocky. We can't all swan round like we're David Essex.

**2** It's the little things that count. Not wiping your nose on your sleeve, stifling your farts so that they seep out quietly. It's difficult, isn't it? But you've got to take the trouble. When she's gone you can let rip, enjoy yourself.

**3** Be polite. It's no good just going up to someone and saying 'Hi darling, can I shag you?' It don't work, I've tried it. You've got to sweet talk them: 'Hello, what's your name? My name's Paul, can I shag you, please?'

**4** Safe sex is very important. Take precautions. Put your fag out. Move your cans where they won't get knocked over.

**5** Foreplay is important. Tease them: they like to be teased. Have a bit of a nap. Put some toast on. Get her to give you a shout when she's ready.

**6** Remember their name. Write it down. On their back if need be. I always keep a biro by the bed. Keep using their name to lock it in your memory. 'You've got nice tits, Denise'; 'You've got a nice arse, Denise'; 'Will you suck me knob, Denise?' Make it personal.

**7** Food can be very sexy. Eat some melted chocolate off her tummy, or ice-cream, or Ready Brek. I had a full English breakfast the other day: eggs, bacon, beans, tomatoes, sausage, black pudding, mushrooms, slice of fried bread, two slices of toast and a cup of tea. She was a big girl.

**8** Role play, that's good: where you pretend to be someone when you're having sex. You could pretend to be a motor mechanic and she could pretend to be a Ford Escort with a flat battery, or something like that. It might be a faulty alternator. Get underneath, have a look.

# Paul's Puzzle

## Help Paul find his pint.

It is a Saturday night and at the end of a pub crawl Paul has lost track of his friends. He vaguely remembers one of them mentioning that there's a lock-in at the Dog's Head, where Paul knows there is a pint waiting for him. Though the locale is familiar to Paul, his orienteering skills have been severely impeded as a result of his having had a skinful. Through state-of-the-art computer technology we are able to simulate the puzzle that presents itself in Paul's head. Paul has ten minutes before the doors are locked.

Handicap yourself to Paul's level by:
- *allowing yourself only 30 seconds to complete the puzzle or*
- *drinking 9 pints.*

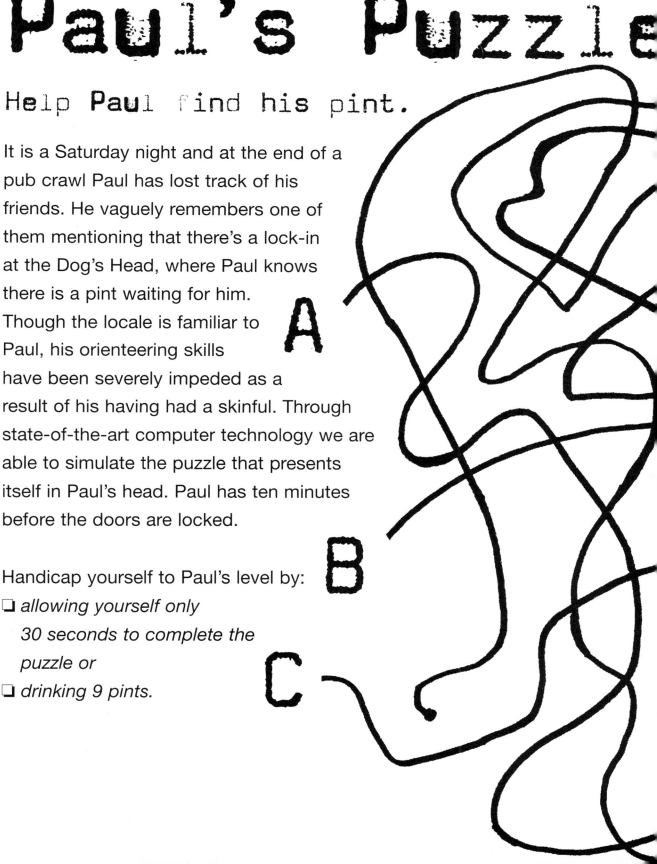

# Page

# PAUL CALF'S
# FANTASTIC

**Hawk Lager** Hawk Lager Hawk Lager

DID YOU KNOW? THE FIRST MOTOR CAR WAS INVENTED BY THE ANCIENT EGYPTIANS. IF YOU DECIPHER THE HIEROGLYPHICS FROM INSIDE TUTANKHAMEN'S TOMB YOU COME UP WITH THE EXACT SPECIFICATION FOR THE VOLKSWAGEN POLO.

OHIO LAGER BEER

5% Volume

THE OHIO PORKER ™
BREWED IN AKRON, OHIO

**DID YOU KNOW**
Albino people are from ou
space but there has bee
a government conspira
to cover it up because they
are quite friendly and pose
no threat. It is worth not-
ing that an albino has
never been elected
President of the
United States of
America.

6% VOL

17

# O'MALLEY'S
### BEST IRISH STOUT

**DID YOU KNOW?**
There is no such thing as the Welsh language. They make it up as they go along to annoy English people.

## STEAM BEER

6% Vol

### EDWARDS
#### OF MANCHESTER

**DID YOU KNOW?**
WG Grace was a woman. The MCC knew all about it but kept quiet so long as the runs kept coming.

## PILSNER LAGER
# BREMEN
### DID YOU KNOW?

During WW2 a Japanese pilot crashed in the Himalayas. He survived alone for 4 months. When they found him by the wreckage he was still alive but he'd lost both his legs. When asked how he had managed to find food all this time he simply raised his remaining arm and pointed to where his limbs had been and screamed 'I ate my legs!'

# FACTS

## SOLEIL

**IMPORTED BRAZILIAN LAGER 5% VOL**

### DID YOU KNOW?

Cockroaches will survive a nuclear holocaust because they are dinosaurs and have been around since the beginning of time. Their shells are impenetrable and, apart from standing on them, they can only be killed by Amazonian blow darts when they are in flight and their backs are exposed.

## OLD BASTARD'S

# DEAD SHEEP BRAINS

1993 VINTAGE 12% VOL

### DID YOU KNOW?

Soil is dead skin. It has accumulated over millions of years from the bodies of people who have died in their sleep.

## BISHOP'S

# BILGE WATER

### BEST MILD BITTER

### DID YOU KNOW?

Cola is well known as a cleaning agent. What people don't know is that if you place a metal knife inside a bottle of Cola for two weeks it will completely dissolve. This had a catastrophic effect when a consignment of Cola burst in the hull of a transatlantic liner, sinking the ship, at the cost of over 1,500 lives. There was a complete cover up by Cola who were worried it would affect their world-wide image and make a mockery of their slogan, 'Cola is life'. Instead, they blamed an iceberg for the sinking of the ship they called the Titanic.

## BIÈRE D'ALSACE

### DID YOU KNOW?

If you dropped a ten pence piece off the top of the Eiffel Tower it would be travelling at twice the speed of sound by the time it reached the pavement below. If it hit a man on the head, the force would be enough to slice him in two like a cheese wire without him having heard a sound.

## BEST BROWN ALE

**Brewed and bottled in Hulme, Manchester**

### DID YOU KNOW?

If a roaring lion comes running towards you in the jungle you must never run away. You must stand your ground and stare it out. As the lion approaches, reach out and, with the nuckle of your middle finger, press firmly between its eyes. Amazingly, the lion will simply lie down and die.

61

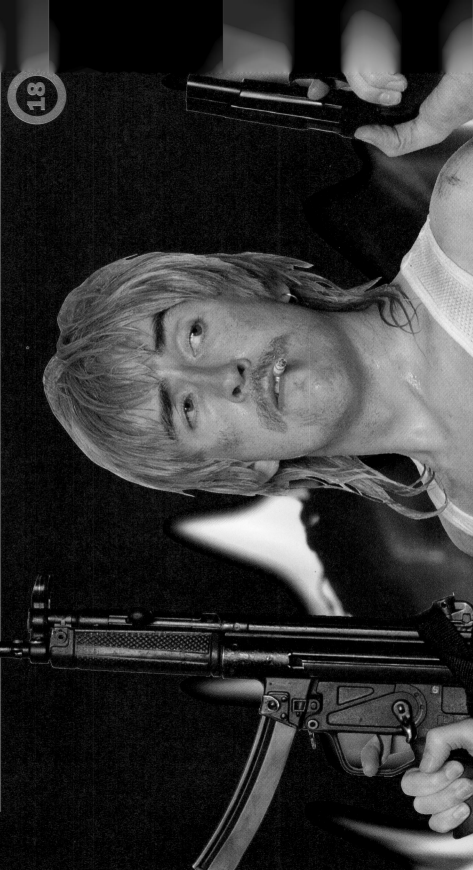

# DEADHARD

## BE AFRAID... BE VERY AFRAID... Y'S**THOUSE

18

PAUL CALF ENTERTAINMENT PRESENTS A PAUL CALF FILM IN ASSOCIATION WITH FAT BOB

# STARRING PAUL CALF · FAT BOB · DARREN LITTLE
## AND PAULINE CALF AS EVA PERON

WRITER: WILL SELF · PRODUCER: ANDREW MACDONALD · DIRECTOR: JANE CAMPION

63

Dear Julie

I can't stop thinking about you. We had some good times and bad times. Do you remember when I was sick in the back of that taxi and he threw us out in the middle of the Peak District at two in the morning and all we had was half a can of lager? And there were bad times as well. Like when we didn't have any lager at all.

Yesterday I found your boob tube in the ~~book~~ boot of the Cortina. I remember the last time you wore it. It was the night I was set upon by five students and I f\*\*\*ing leathered the lot of them. Why can't it always be like that?

I'll never forget that look on your face that night, shagging in the back of my car. I wish it had been me. I want you to know I will change. I'm trying to give up two of my worst habits — smoking and masturbation — which I'm finding difficult as I'm a twenty a day man — and I smoke like a chimney.

Paul

Greetings from
the Peak District

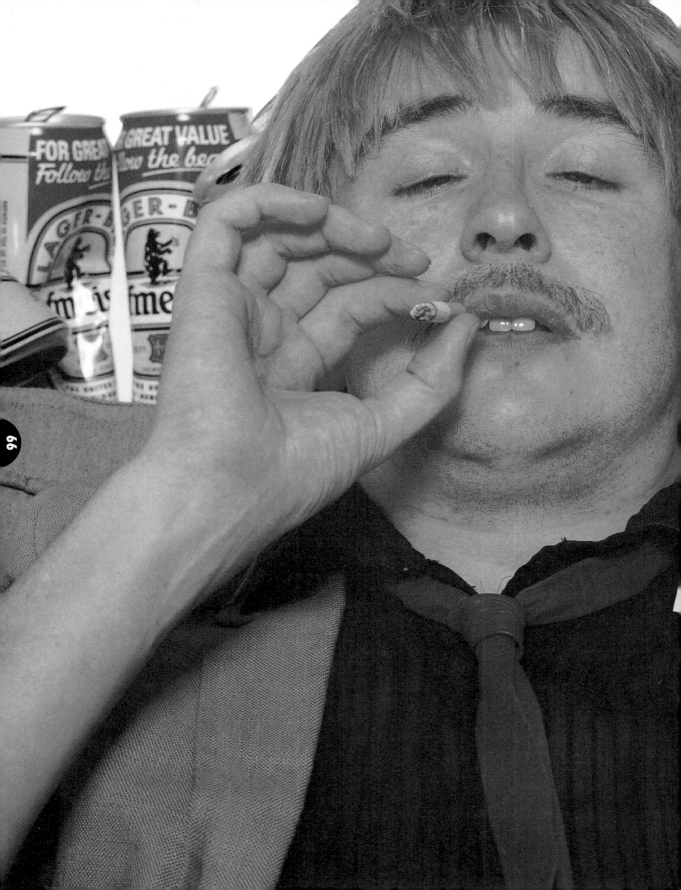

# PAUL'S TOP TEN FILMS

1. Gumball Rally
2. Our Man Flint
3. Showgirls
4. Rambo 3
5. Police Academy
6. Carry on Camping
7. Taste the Blood of Dracula
8. Confessions of a Window Cleaner
9. Scum
10. Black Emanuelle

# ARE YOU A

*1* You are sitting in a Genito-urinary Clinic chatting with the regulars and browsing through a guide to 'What's On Locally in the World of Arts and Entertainment' when you come across a full-page advert for a forthcoming season of films by Polish Cinematographer, Krzysztof Kieślowski.

## DO YOU ?

❏ Find it hard to contain yourself and enthusiastically describe the directorial subtleties of the Three Colours trilogy to the man sitting next to you, insisting that he familiarise himself with Kieślowski's work. [1]

❏ Turn the page. [3]

❏ Hold it up to the person next to you and say, 'Is there much shagging in his stuff ?' [6]

*2* You wake up and realise you have half an hour before you need to leave the house for a job interview.

## DO YOU ?

❏ Start running around like a blue-arsed fly, tarting yourself up, all ponsified and combing your hair like a girl. [1]

❏ Get up at the last minute. Scratch your arse. Pull on some tight stonewash jeans. Turn up late at the interview and punch your prospective employer. [3]

❏ Have a wank and go back to sleep for another three hours. [6]

*3* It is the end of a romantic evening at the dog track. You've been getting on very well. Naturally you invite your lady friend back for a shag. She politely declines, saying 'Not on the first date', but says she would like to see you again.

## DO YOU ?

❏ Feel bad about having asked her back. She's better than that and deserves more respect. [1]

❏ Hit the roof, claim you spent £6.50 on her ticket and that you don't get something for nothing. Ask her who does she think she is, Princess Di? [3]

❏ Say you understand perfectly and that you look forward to seeing her later in the week. Then, after dropping her off, go and get pissed and pick a fight. [5]

❏ Check round the back of the Dog's Head to see if Big Bertha's there. [6]

*4* You are sitting at a crowded bar when a student nudges you, spilling your drink.

## DO YOU ?

❏ Ignore him. [3]

❏ Move away, giving him space to get through whilst making some friendly comment like, 'Are you alright there mate?' [1]

❏ Stare him out for the next hour. When he goes to the toilet, follow him, piss on his shoes, then offer him an olive branch by letting him buy you a pint. [6]

# PAUL CALF?

**5** You are sick in the back of a taxi.

### DO YOU ?

❏ Apologise profusely. Say that this has never happened before and offer to pay to have the seat cleaned professionally. [1]

❏ Hope the driver hasn't noticed and try to disguise your indiscretion by staring out of the window and humming a happy tune. [3]

❏ Get rid of the remaining sick on your hand by wiping it on the seat. Then, as you catch the eye of the driver in the rear view mirror, say 'What the f*** are you looking at?' [6]

**6** You are driving along a dual carriage way when you are flashed by a speed camera.

### DO YOU ?

❏ Hit the steering wheel cursing your idiocy and the inevitability of the imminent arrival of three fixed penalty points through the post, ultimately accepting that you were caught fair and square. [1]

❏ Think of various scams to avoid being penalised, e.g. claiming the car was stolen or that a friend was driving the car (Fat Bob). [3]

❏ Drive home and return an hour later with bolt cutters and oxyaccetalene blow lamp. Remove the speed camera, put it in the back of your car, before dumping it in a reservoir at Saddleworth Moor. [6]

**7** You wake up to find yourself in a multi-storey car park stairwell. You smell of piss, one of your shoes has been thrown onto the roof of an adjacent building and is irretrievable, your nose is bloodied and you have cuts and bruises.

### DO YOU ?

❏ Go to the nearest door and ask them to call the police, explaining that you are upset and bewildered. [1]

❏ Sit with your head in your hands, weeping 'How did I get into this terrible state? Where have I gone wrong with my life?' [3]

❏ Walk home, have a bowl of Sugar Puffs, made with water, and go to bed. [6]

69

# The Instant Calf Family

Recreate the Calf household by simply donning the masks and having ill-informed conversations of little or no consequence.

## Instant Paul

Cut along dotted line. Tie string in holes at side. Dress badly.